T0183231

Lecture Notes in Computer Science 14210

Founding Editors

Gerhard Goos
Juris Hartmanis

Editorial Board Members

Elisa Bertino, *Purdue University, West Lafayette, IN, USA*
Wen Gao, *Peking University, Beijing, China*
Bernhard Steffen , *TU Dortmund University, Dortmund, Germany*
Moti Yung , *Columbia University, New York, NY, USA*

The series Lecture Notes in Computer Science (LNCS), including its subseries Lecture Notes in Artificial Intelligence (LNAI) and Lecture Notes in Bioinformatics (LNBI), has established itself as a medium for the publication of new developments in computer science and information technology research, teaching, and education.

LNCS enjoys close cooperation with the computer science R & D community, the series counts many renowned academics among its volume editors and paper authors, and collaborates with prestigious societies. Its mission is to serve this international community by providing an invaluable service, mainly focused on the publication of conference and workshop proceedings and postproceedings. LNCS commenced publication in 1973.

Sheng He · Jiacai Lai · Liang-Jie Zhang
Editors

Metaverse – METAVERSE 2023

19th International Conference
Held as Part of the Services Conference Federation, SCF 2023
Honolulu, HI, USA, September 23–26, 2023
Proceedings

Springer

Editors
Sheng He ⓘ
Kingdee Software Group Co., Ltd
Shenzhen, China

Jiacai Lai
Lecheng Times Technology Co., Ltd
Beijing, China

Liang-Jie Zhang ⓘ
Shenzhen Enterpreneurship and Innovation
Federation (SEIF)
Shenzhen, China

ISSN 0302-9743   ISSN 1611-3349 (electronic)
Lecture Notes in Computer Science
ISBN 978-3-031-44753-2   ISBN 978-3-031-44754-9 (eBook)
https://doi.org/10.1007/978-3-031-44754-9

This Springer imprint is published by the registered company Springer Nature Switzerland AG
The registered company address is: Gewerbestrasse 11, 6330 Cham, Switzerland

Paper in this product is recyclable.

Preface

To rapidly respond to the changing economy, the World Congress on Services has been naturally extended to become the International Conference on Metaverse to cover immersive services for all vertical industries and area solutions. With the emergence of Metaverse, the current services will be gradually transformed into immersive services that construct digital worlds and connect with physical worlds. The immersive services are the core characteristics of Metaverse.

This volume presents the accepted papers for the 2023 International Conference on Metaverse (METAVERSE 2023) held as a hybrid conference during September 23–26, 2023 On-Site in Honolulu, Hawaii, USA with Satellite Sessions in Shenzhen, Guangdong, China and also Online for those could not attend on-site. All topics concerned Metaverse engineering foundations and applications, with a focus on novel approaches for engineering requirements, design and architectures, testing, maintenance and evolution, model-driven development, software processes, metrics, quality assurance and new software economics models, and search-based software engineering, benefiting the day-to-day services sectors and derived from experience, with appreciation of scale, pragmatism, transparency, compliance, and/or dependability.

We accepted 9 papers, including 6 full papers and 3 short papers, from 15 submissions. Each was reviewed and selected by at least three independent members of the METAVERSE 2023 International Program Committee in a single-blind review process. We are pleased to thank the authors whose submissions and participation made this conference possible. We also want to express our thanks to the Program Committee members, for their dedication in helping to organize the conference and reviewing the submissions. We owe special thanks to the keynote speakers for their impressive speeches.

August 2023

Sheng He
Jiacai Lai
Liang-Jie Zhang

Organization

Conference Committees

Program Chairs

Sheng He   Kingdee International Software Group Co., Ltd, China

Application Track Chair

Jiacai Lai   Lecheng Times Techonology Co., Ltd., China

Services Conference Federation (SCF 2023)

General Chairs

Ali Arsanjani   Google, USA
Wu Chou   Essenlix Corporation, USA

Program Chair

Liang-Jie Zhang   Shenzhen Entrepreneurship and Innovation Federation, China

CFO

Min Luo   Georgia Tech, USA

Operation Committee

Jing Zeng   China Gridcom Co., Ltd., China
Yishuang Ning   Tsinghua University, China
Sheng He   Tsinghua University, China

Steering Committee

Calton Pu (Co-chair)	Georgia Tech, USA
Liang-Jie Zhang (Co-chair)	Shenzhen Entrepreneurship and Innovation Federation, China

METAVERSE 2023 Program Committee

Huihui Chen	Foshan University, China
Ben Falchuk	Peraton Labs, USA
Xinxin Fan	IoTeX, USA
Chao Li	Beijing Jiaotong University, China
Zhenjiang Li	City University of Hong Kong, China
Jia Liu	Nanjing University, China
Stefano Sebastio	Raytheon Technologies, Ireland
Chuyu Wang	Nanjing University, China
Kunjing Zhang	China Academy of Information and Communications Technology, China
Yanchao Zhao	Nanjing University of Aeronautics and Astronautics, China
Waseem Mufti	Benazir Bhutto Shaheed University, Pakistan
Vikas Shah	Knights of Columbus, USA
Ge Wang	Xi'an Jiaotong University, China
Xiaohu Fan	Wuhan Collage, China
Bin Tang	Hohai University, China
Pengfei Wang	Dalian University of Technology, China
Shigeng Zhang	Central South University, China

Conference Sponsor – Services Society

The Services Society (S2) is a non-profit professional organization that has been created to promote worldwide research and technical collaboration in services innovations among academia and industrial professionals. Its members are volunteers from industry and academia with common interests. S2 is registered in the USA as a "501(c) organization", which means that it is an American tax-exempt nonprofit organization. S2 collaborates with other professional organizations to sponsor or co-sponsor conferences and to promote an effective services curriculum in colleges and universities. S2 initiates and promotes a "Services University" program worldwide to bridge the gap between industrial needs and university instruction.

The Services Sector accounts for 79.5% of the GDP of the USA in 2016. The Services Society has formed 5 Special Interest Groups (SIGs) to support technology- and domain-specific professional activities.

- Special Interest Group on Services Computing (SIG-SC)
- Special Interest Group on Big Data (SIG-BD)
- Special Interest Group on Cloud Computing (SIG-CLOUD)
- Special Interest Group on Artificial Intelligence (SIG-AI)
- Special Interest Group on Metaverse (SIG-Metaverse)

About the Services Conference Federation (SCF)

As the founding member of the Services Conference Federation (SCF), the first International Conference on Web Services (ICWS) was held in June 2003 in Las Vegas, USA. Meanwhile, the First International Conference on Web Services - Europe 2003 (ICWS-Europe 2003) was held in Germany in October 2003. ICWS-Europe 2003 was an extended event of the 2003 International Conference on Web Services (ICWS 2003) in Europe. In 2004, ICWS-Europe was changed to the European Conference on Web Services (ECOWS), which was held at Erfurt, Germany.

2023 Services Conference Federation (SCF 2023, http://www.icws.org/) was a hybrid conference On-Site in Honolulu, Hawaii, USA, with Satellite Sessions in Shenzhen, Guangdong, China and also Online for those could not attend on-site. All the virtual conference presentations were given via pre-recorded videos during September 23-26, 2023 through the BigMarker Video Broadcasting Platform: https://www.bigmarker.com/series/services-conference-federati/series_summit

To present a new form and improve the impact of the conference, we also planned an Automatic Webinar which was presented by experts in various fields. All the invited talks were given via pre-recorded videos and broadcast in a live-like form recursively by two session channels during the conference period. Each invited talk was converted into an on-demand webinar right after the conference.

In the past 20 years, the ICWS community has expanded from Web engineering innovations to scientific research for the whole services industry. Service delivery platforms have been expanded to mobile platforms, Internet of Things, cloud computing, and edge computing. The services ecosystem has gradually been enabled, value added, and intelligence embedded through enabling technologies such as big data, artificial intelligence, and cognitive computing. In the coming years, all transactions with multiple parties involved will be transformed to blockchain.

Based on technology trends and best practices in the field, the Services Conference Federation (SCF) will continue serving as the conference umbrella's code name for all services-related conferences. SCF 2023 defined the future of New ABCDE (AI, Blockchain, Cloud, BigData & IOT). We are very proud to announce that SCF 2023's 10 co-located theme topic conferences all centered around "services", with each focusing on exploring different themes (web-based services, cloud-based services, Big Data-based services, services innovation lifecycle, AI-driven ubiquitous services, blockchain driven trust service-ecosystems, Metaverse services and applications, and emerging service-oriented technologies).

Some highlights of SCF 2023 are shown below:

– **Bigger Platform**: The 10 collocated conferences (SCF 2023) were sponsored by the Services Society, which is the world-leading not-for-profit organization (501 c(3)) dedicated to the service of more than 30,000 worldwide Services Computing researchers and practitioners. A bigger platform means bigger opportunities for all volunteers, authors, and participants. Meanwhile, Springer provided sponsorship to best paper awards and other professional activities. All the 10 conference proceedings of SCF 2023 were published by Springer and indexed in ISI Conference Proceedings Citation Index (included in Web of Science), Engineering Index EI (Compendex and Inspec databases), DBLP, Google Scholar, IO-Port, MathSciNet, Scopus, and ZBlMath.

- **Brighter Future**: While celebrating the 2023 version of ICWS, SCF 2023 highlighted the International Conference on Blockchain (ICBC 2023) and the International Conference on Metaverse (Metaverse 2023) to build the fundamental infrastructure for enabling secure and trusted services ecosystems. This will lead our community members to create their own brighter future.
- **Better Model**: SCF 2023 continued to leverage the invented Conference Blockchain Model (CBM) to innovate the organizing practices for all the 10 theme conferences. Senior researchers in the field are welcome to submit proposals to serve as CBM Ambassador for an individual conference to start better interactions during your leadership role in organizing future SCF conferences.

Member of SCF 2023

The Services Conference Federation (SCF) includes 10 service-oriented conferences: ICWS, CLOUD, SCC, BigData Congress, AIMS, METAVERSE, ICIOT, EDGE, ICCC, and ICBC.

[1] 2023 International Conference on Web Services (ICWS 2023, http://icws.org/2023) was the flagship theme-topic conference for Web-centric services, enabling technologies and applications.

[2] 2023 International Conference on Cloud Computing (CLOUD 2023, http://thecloudcomputing.org/2023) was the flagship theme-topic conference for resource sharing, utility-like usage models, IaaS, PaaS, and SaaS.

[3] 2023 International Conference on Big Data (BigData 2023, http://bigdatacongress.org/2023) was the theme-topic conference for data sourcing, data processing, data analysis, data-driven decision making, and data-centric applications.

[4] 2023 International Conference on Services Computing (SCC 2023, http://thescc.org/2023) was the flagship theme-topic conference for leveraging the latest computing technologies to design, develop, deploy, operate, manage, modernize, and redesign business services.

[5] 2023 International Conference on AI & Mobile Services (AIMS 2023, http://ai1000.org/2023) was the theme-topic conference for artificial intelligence, neural networks, machine learning, training data sets, AI scenarios, AI delivery channels, and AI supporting infrastructure as well as mobile internet services. The goal of AIMS was to bring AI to any mobile devices and other channels.

[6] 2023 International Conference on Metaverse (Metaverse 2023, http://metaverse1000.org/2023) put its focus on all innovations of the services industry, including financial services, education services, transportation services, energy services, government services, manufacturing services, consulting services, and other industry services.

[7] 2023 International Conference on Cognitive Computing (ICCC 2023, http://thecog nitivecomputing.org/2023) put its focus on leveraging the latest computing technologies to simulate, model, implement, and realize cognitive sensing and brain operating systems.

[8] 2023 International Conference on Internet of Things (ICIOT 2023, http://iciot.org/ 2023) put its focus on the science, technology, and applications of IOT device innovations as well as IOT services in various solution scenarios.

[9] 2023 International Conference on Edge Computing (EDGE 2023, http://theedgeco mputing.org/2023) was a theme-topic conference for leveraging the latest computing technologies to enable localized device connections, edge gateways, edge applications, edge-cloud interactions, edge-user experiences, and edge business models.

[10] 2023 International Conference on Blockchain (ICBC 2023, http://blockchain1000. org/2023) concentrated on all aspects of blockchain, including digital currency, distributed application development, industry-specific blockchains, public blockchains, community blockchains, private blockchains, blockchain-based services, and enabling technologies.

Contents

Research Track

CEESys: A Cloud-Edge-End System for Data Acquisition, Transmission and Processing Based on HiSilicon and OpenHarmony

Hongyu Tian[1,2] and Kejiang Ye[1(✉)]

[1] Shenzhen Institute of Advanced Technology,
Chinese Academy of Sciences, Shenzhen 518055, China
{hy.tian1,kj.ye}@siat.ac.cn
[2] University of Chinese Academy of Sciences, Beijing 100049, China

Abstract. In a typical industry environment, temperature, humidity and light intensity are the key environmental parameters. Cloud-Edge-End architecture is perfect to process IoT data. However, the existing solutions are usually developed for particular devices or protocols, causing low development efficiency and poor scalability. In this paper, we design and implement a Cloud-Edge-End System (CEESys) for data acquisition, transmission, and processing based on a unified operating system - OpenHarmony. The main functions of the system include: WiFi configuration with NFC, parameter acquisition of temperature, humidity and light intensity, data transmission, command issuance, etc. To implement the system, we first design a NFC touch function to configure the network, then we use the IoT Device Access (IoTDA) service on the Huawei Cloud IoT Platform in order to connect physical devices to the cloud, and finally collect device data and deliver commands to the device for remote control. The testing results show that the system implements the functions of data acquisition, data transmission through network, command issuing, data visualization and analysis.

Keywords: Internet of Things · Industrial Internet · Edge Computing · HiSilicon · OpenHarmony

1 Introduction

In a typical Internet of Things (IoT) environment such as industrial IoT scenarios, temperature, humidity and light intensity are the key environmental parameters. How to effectively acquire, transmit and process industrial environment data is crucial to provide real-time monitoring of temperature, humidity and light intensity [10], ensuring that industrial products meet quality standards and regulatory requirements, and providing necessary evidence and reports. The importance of industrial environmental monitoring systems is summarized as follows:

© The Author(s), under exclusive license to Springer Nature Switzerland AG 2023
S. He et al. (Eds.): METAVERSE 2023, LNCS 14210, pp. 3–14, 2023.
https://doi.org/10.1007/978-3-031-44754-9_1

- Industrial environmental monitoring systems can be applied to monitor the condition in the storage and transportation environment in real time, help protect industrial products from temperature, humidity or light fluctuations and providing accurate records and traceability;
- By monitoring the working environment of industrial equipment, it can timely identify potential problems and take preventive measures to avoid industrial equipment failures;
- Industrial environmental monitoring systems have the ability to collect a large amount of data, which can be combined with other information and data for further analysis.

Currently, IoT applications generally adopt the classic three-layer architecture, including the perception layer, the network layer, the application and the service layer [5]. Base on this architecture, service providers such as Amazon, Google, and Microsoft have proposed their own cloud platform solutions for IoT [23]. However, at present, most of the IoT cloud platform solutions do not have unified operating system support, the implementation methods of each layer are relatively independent, the system integration process is relatively complex, and the efficiency of system development and deployment is relatively low. With HarmonyOS as the core, recently Huawei provides an access-independent, safe, reliable, open and flexible IoT cloud platform solution [20]. Originated from HarmonyOS, OpenHarmony is committed to building an open, globally leading distributed operating system for multiple intelligent terminals and full scenarios, and building a sustainable open source ecosystem. OpenHarmony can adapt to the HiSilicon Hi3861 development board, which is released by Huawei and is based on the RISC-V [28] architecture.

In this paper, we design and implement a Cloud-Edge-End System (CEESys) for data acquisition, transmission, and processing based on HiSilicon and OpenHarmony. The main functions of the system include: WiFi configuration with NFC [27], temperature, humidity and light intensity parameter acquisition, data transmission, command issuance, etc. The innovation of system include:

- Many traditional IoT cloud solutions [2,7] are based on database such as MySQL, and have high difficulty, high cost, and low efficiency in developing, expanding, and maintaining multiple communication protocols. Thus, we choose Huawei Cloud IoT services to simplify the difficulty of device access. Huawei Cloud IoT services widely support standard IoT access protocols and private protocols, meet the requirements of various devices and access scenarios, and provide plug-in mechanisms to achieve custom protocol resolution.
- Previously, the popular Edge device operating system was generally based on Linux [13,15], and was difficult to adapt and deploy on different terminal devices. Therefore, we choose the open-source distributed OpenHarmony-v3.0-LTS as the operating system, which adopted a component-based design scheme. It can be flexibly tailored according to the resource capabilities and business characteristics of the device to meet the requirements of different terminal devices for operating systems and provides multiple lightweight network protocols, a lightweight graphics framework, and a wide range of read/write components with the IoT bus.

- The hardware platform is different from the traditional platforms such as C51, NodeMCU, STM32 [18] and Raspberry Pi. We use Hi3861V100 as the main control chip that can run OpenHarmony perfectly, Hi3861V100 has the advantages of rich interfaces, low power consumption, and stable performance.
- It is simple, convenient, and flexible to use NFC to configure device networks in industrial scenarios, so NFC touch function is designed to configure the network and connect physical devices to the cloud, and collect device data and deliver commands to the device for remote control.

The reminder of this paper is organized as follows: In Sect. 2, we present the related works in environmental monitoring system. The architecture of the whole system is introduced in Sect. 3. In Sect. 4, we describe the design and implementation of hardware and software in detail. In Sect. 5, we test the system locally and in the cloud platform, respectively. Finally the conclusions are given in Sect. 6.

2 Related Works

Zhang et al. [31] propose a smart agriculture system based on the multi-source data fusion model, BearPi-HM Nano and Huawei Harmony OS, improving the performance and efficiency of intelligent scheduling of agricultural production. In [7], the authors implement a cloud platform for the acquisition of data from various sensors. The sensor signals acquired by the ESP32 microcontroller (MCU) are collected by the Raspberry Pi serving as the edge device and then published with the DDS application to the cloud and stored to the MySQL database. Xiao et al. [29] designed an intelligent real-time temperature and humidity monitoring system based on ZigBee wireless network communication technology and ESP8266 WiFi technology. Kumar et al. [15] and Khot et al. [13] introduce a real-time remote light intensity monitoring system using the Raspberry Pi which enables the user to track the lighting system remotely. The main characteristic of the proposed system is timely light intensity monitoring and storage of data in the database on the cloud for future reference. In [2], smart data acquisition devices are designed and developed through which energy data are transferred to the edge IIoT servers, these servers can exchange data through a secured message queuing telemetry transport protocol. Edge and cloud databases are used to handle big data. The authors in [25] develop an arrangement that encompasses Arduino wireless sensor networks and the cloud, and then extend their work to develop a method for data transmission between them, which can be of great use in monitoring temperature and humidity. In [30], the central air conditioning energy consumption monitoring and optimization application based on the INDICS platform and the intelligent gateway SMART IOT edge was introduced. Despite these works, data acquisition, transmission and processing systems for temperature, humidity, light intensity, etc. have been implemented based on different Cloud-Edge-End solutions. However, there is no complete bottom-up IoT solution from the device end to the cloud platform and the user end, the efficiency of system development and deployment has the potential to be improved.

3   CEESys Architecture

The CEESys is designed based on a three-layer architecture of Cloud, Edge and End.

- The end layer uses Hi3861V100 as the main control chip and uses I2C [9] bus to communicate with the SHT20 temperature and humidity sensor, the AP3216C light sensor, the PCF8547 chip and the SSD1306 chip to collect environmental parameters, send control signals to the small DC fan and display real-time data on the OLED screen.
- The edge layer uses the TCP/IP protocol to receive the collected data from the end layer through WiFi [6] and then uses the MQTT protocol to communicate with the application and service layer.
- The cloud layer can not only monitor and display light intensity, temperature and humidity of the industrial environment in real time, but also issue commands to control the working state of the fan. The user can also observe the data visualization result in the data analysis page, to perform a more intuitive analysis.

The overall architecture of the system is shown in Fig. 1.

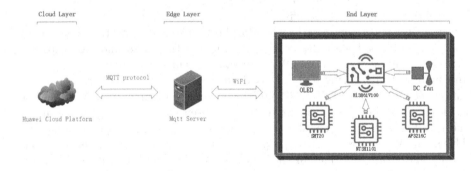

Fig. 1. CEESys architecture

4   System Design and Implementation

4.1   System Hardware

The system hardware consists of a Hi3861V100 main control chip, the SHT20 sensor, the AP3216 sensor, the small DC fan controlled by PCF8574, the NT3H1101 chip used for NFC, and the OLED screen driven by SSD1306. The main control chip communicates with other modules through the I2C bus, which is a popular serial data transfer protocol and is widely used. Table 1 gives a summary of the hardware devices.

Table 1. Hardware devices

Model Number	Type	Function
Hi3861V100	Main control chip	Provide general control signals and WiFi connection
SHT20	Sensor	Collect temperature and humidity
AP3216C	Sensor	Collect light intensity
PCF8574	IO expansion chip	Control small DC fan
NT3H1101	NFC card chip	NFC tag and responder
SSD1306	Single-chip driver	Drive OLED display

- **Hi3861V100.** Hi3861V100 WiFi baseband supports orthogonal frequency division multiplexing (OFDM) [17] technology, backward compatibility direct-sequence spread-spectrum (DSSS) [19], and complementary code keying (CCK) [11] technology, and supports various data rates of the IEEE 802.11 b/g/n protocol. The Hi3861V100 chip integrates a high performance 32bit microprocessor, a hardware security engine, and rich peripheral interfaces, including SPI [16], UART [21], I2C, PWM [8], GPIO [1], and multichannel ADC. It also supports high-speed SDIO [14] 2.0 slave interface, with a maximum clock of 50MHz; The chip has built-in SRAM and Flash, which can run independently and support running programs on Flash. Hi3861V100 supports OpenHarmony LiteOS-M and third-party components, and provides an open and easy-to-use development and debugging environment [26].
- **SHT20.** The SHT20 sensor contains a capacitive type humidity sensor, a band-gap temperature sensor, and specialized analog and digital integrated circuit - all on a single CMOSens chip [22]. SHT20 can provide extremely high reliability and excellent long-term stability, with the advantages of low power consumption, fast response, strong anti-interference ability and high accuracy. The sensor has an error of only $\pm$ 2% RH at 10% RH to 90% RH (at 25 °C), and an error of only $\pm$ 0.2 °C at 0 to 65 °C (typical value).
- **AP3216C.** The AP3216C is an integrated ALS & PS module that includes a digital ambient light sensor, a proximity sensor, and an IR LED in a single package. The ALS provides 16-bit effective linear output of light intensity, range from 0 to 65535.
- **PCF8574.** On the development board, the PCF8574 I/O expansion chip is used to control the small DC fan. Through the I2C bus, PCF8574 sends status to Hi3861 or receives commands from Hi3861.
- **NT3H1101.** NFC communication uses the NT3H1101 chip produced by NXP Corporation. This chip supports I2C communication, supports configurable on-site detection pins, and is internally equipped with an EEPROM storage chip, allowing fast data transfer between RF and I2C without limiting the write cycle of EEPROM memory.
- **SSD1306.** SSD1306 is a single-chip CMOS OLED/PLED driver with controller for the organic/polymer light-emitting diode dot-matrix graphic display system.

4.2 System Software

– **OpenHarmony.** The OpenHarmony LiteOS-M kernel has the advantages of being small in size, having low power consumption, and high performance. The development of this system is based on the kernel abstraction layer, which provides task scheduling, memory management, communication mechanism, interrupt exception, time management and software timer functions. The version of OpenHarmony source code is OpenHarmony-v3.0-LTS, the complete development process is based on the DevEco Device Tool, an integrated development environment (IDE), which is used for one-stop development, covering dependency installation, building, burning, and running. The development process is shown in Fig. 2.
– **WiFi and NFC.** NFC's Ndef [24] communication protocol is used between the mobile end and the device end. It uses a mobile program to transfer WiFi hotspot information to the on-board WiFi module through NFC and then configures the hotspot information to connect the device to the specified WiFi hotspot. Finally, the device obtains the IP through the DHCP protocol and successfully connects to the network. The WiFi connect process is shown in Fig. 3.
– **MQTT.** As a lightweight protocol based on a publish and subscribe communication mode, MQTT can transmit data from one to many and is suitable for the distributed characteristic of OpenHarmony. MQTT is also based on the client server mode and built on top of the TCP/IP protocol, which can greatly decouple applications [4]. MQTT will build an underlying network transmission, which establishes an orderly, lossless, byte stream based bidirectional transmission channel between the client and server [12]. Figure 4 shows the MQTT process, as a client of the MQTT protocol, the relevant business

Fig. 2. OpenHarmony development process

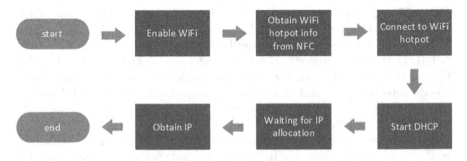

Fig. 3. WiFi connection

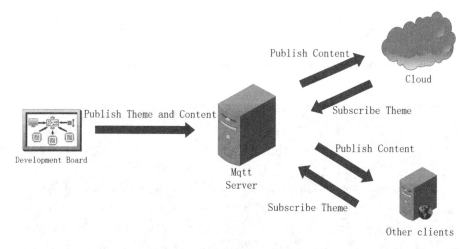

Fig. 4. MQTT protocol

code needs to be organized on the development board, mainly including the definition of the network connection information structure, the MQTT client information structure, the initialization of the MQTT client, the MQTT client connection proxy server, the subscription to the MQTT messages, the distribution of the MQTT messages, etc. In this paper, we adopt Huawei Cloud's MQTT proxy server, and these codes are designed using third-party code from the OpenHarmony project.

– **Huawei cloud platform.** The Huawei IoT device access cloud service provides access and management capabilities for massive devices, connecting physical devices to the cloud, supporting device data collection, and sending commands to the cloud for remote control [3]. To implement connection, data push and command reception between the device end and the cloud platform, the cloud platform configuration is necessary: register and log in to the Huawei cloud platform, apply device access to IoTDA, create products, register devices, create product models, add specific services, and define attributes and commands in each service. Then write the MQTT ClientId, username and password generated, as well as the IP address of the MQTT server on the Huawei cloud platform, in the underlying code of the board to achieve interconnection between the board and the cloud platform.

5 System Testing

5.1 Local Test

In local test experiment, we first turn on the Hi3861 development board, then communicate with the PC through serial port, and capture output information at the serial port terminal. As shown in Fig. 5, the system is able to obtain environmental parameter information including light intensity, temperature and humidity normally. At the same time, the temperature, humidity, and light intensity of the current environment are displayed in real-time on the OLED screen, as shown in Fig. 6, the titles in yellow correspond to the parameters in blue.

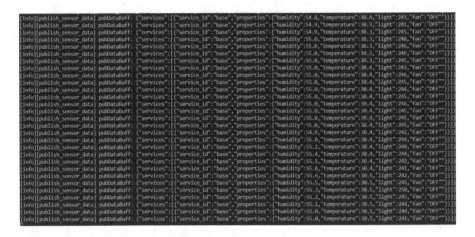

Fig. 5. The result from serial port terminal

5.2   Cloud Service Test

In cloud service test experiment, we first create a product on the Huawei cloud platform and specify the communication protocol type as MQTT protocol. Then we add service attributes such as temperature, humidity, light intensity, fan status, and commands for controlling the switch of fan peripherals. After that, we register the device and obtain the device ID and the device key. We modify the configuration file based on the above information and then move the mobile with an NFC program closer to the onboard NFC coil and transmit the WiFi hotspot information to the device to enable the device to connect to the network.

To artificially simulate environmental changes near sensors, we slowly approach the heat source to the sensor, create airflow to affect air humidity, and occasionally block the light sensor. We can use the cloud platform to observe the changes in temperature, humidity, and light intensity uploaded, as shown in Fig. 7. By comparing data on the cloud platform with PC serial terminal output, it can be seen that the results are consistent. By issuing control fan on and off instructions from the cloud, the fan changes its working state according to the control commands.

In order to monitor data changes more intuitively, we use the line chart and heat map of real-time data statistics, as shown in Fig. 8 and Fig. 9, the green line represents humidity, the blue line represents temperature, and the purple line represents light intensity, time interval is 1 s.

Fig. 6. The result displayed in OLED screen

Fig. 7. The result displayed in Huawei cloud platform

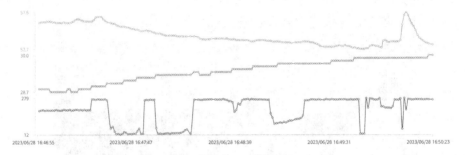

Fig. 8. The line chart of environment parameter changes (green represents humidity, blue represents temperature, purple represents light intensity, time interval is 1 s) (Color figure online)

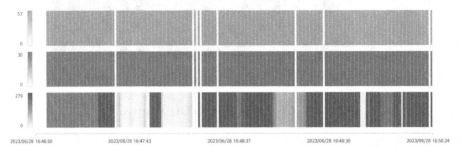

Fig. 9. The heat map of environment parameter changes (green represents humidity, blue represents temperature, purple represents light intensity, time interval is 1 s) (Color figure online)

6   Conclusion

In this paper, we design and implement a Cloud-Edge-End System (CEESys) for data acquisition, transmission and processing based on HiSilicon and OpenHarmony. The hardware uses the Hi3861 development board based on the RISC-V architecture, and the software is developed on the OpenHarmony LiteOS-M kernel. During testing, the sensor data is real-time uploaded to the cloud through the MQTT protocol, and instructions are issued to control the working status of the fan. Finally, the temperature, humidity and light intensity data are visualized in the cloud by means of line chart and heat map. The testing results show that the system implement the functions of data acquisition, data transmission through network, command issuing, data visualization and analysis. Compared to other IoT solutions, adopting Cloud-Edge-End architecture and using Open-Harmony to design and develop an industrial environment monitoring system has improved system development efficiency and rapid system deployment. CEESys not only enables remote real-time monitoring of industry environments, but also enables effective management through remote control. In the future, we will further improve the functions and will also develop OpenHarmony-based mobile applications.

Acknowledgment. This work is supported by the National Key R&D Program of China (No. 2021YFB3300200), National Natural Science Foundation of China (No. 62072451, 92267105), Guangdong Special Support Plan (No. 2021TQ06X990), Shenzhen Basic Research Program (No. JCYJ20200109115418592, JCYJ20220818101610023), Zhejiang Lab Open Research Project (No. K2022NB0AB01).

References

1. Balachandran, S.: General purpose input output (gpio). Michigan State University College of Engineering. Published, pp. 08–11 (2009)
2. Bin Mofidul, R., Alam, M.M., Rahman, M.H., Jang, Y.M.: Real-time energy data acquisition, anomaly detection, and monitoring system: Implementation of a secured, robust, and integrated global iiot infrastructure with edge and cloud ai. Sensors **22**(22) (2022). https://doi.org/10.3390/s22228980. https://www.mdpi.com/1424-8220/22/22/8980
3. Chen, J., Hu, K., Wang, Q., Sun, Y., Shi, Z., He, S.: Narrowband internet of things: implementations and applications. IEEE Internet Things J. **4**(6), 2309–2314 (2017)
4. Cui, P.: Comparison of IoT application layer protocols. Ph.D. thesis, Auburn University (2017)
5. Duan, R., Chen, X., Xing, T.: A qos architecture for iot. In: 2011 International Conference on Internet of Things and 4th International Conference on Cyber, Physical and Social Computing, pp. 717–720. IEEE (2011)
6. Forouzan, B.A.: TCP/IP protocol suite. McGraw-Hill Higher Education (2002)
7. Ho, M.H., Yen, H.C., Lai, M.Y., Liu, Y.T.: Implementation of dds cloud platform for real-time data acquisition of sensors. In: 2021 International Symposium on Intelligent Signal Processing and Communication Systems (ISPACS)m pp. 1–2 (2021). https://doi.org/10.1109/ISPACS51563.2021.9650986
8. Holtz, J.: Advanced pwm and predictive control-an overview. IEEE Trans. Industr. Electron. **63**(6), 3837–3844 (2015)
9. Hu, Z.w.: I2c protocol design for reusability. In: 2010 Third International Symposium on Information Processing, pp. 83–86. IEEE (2010)
10. Jaber, A.A., Al-Mousawi, F.K.I., Jasem, H.S.: Internet of things based industrial environment monitoring and control: a design approach. Int. J. Electr. Comput. Eng. (IJECE) **9**(6), 4657–4667 (2019)
11. Jeong, W., Park, H.: A cck-ofdm modem having low peak-to-average power ratio. In: ITC-CSCC: International Technical Conference on Circuits Systems, Computers and Communications, pp. 1539–1542 (2003)
12. Ji, H., Sun, S., Xie, Y., Liu, H., Jiang, T.: Research and application of internet of things edge autonomy technology based on microservice in power pipe gallary. In: 2020 7th International Conference on Information Science and Control Engineering (ICISCE), pp. 2062–2066. IEEE (2020)
13. Khot, S.B., Gaikwad, M.: Development of cloud-based light intensity monitoring system for green house using raspberry pi. In: 2016 International Conference on Computing Communication Control and automation (ICCUBEA), pp. 1–4. IEEE (2016)
14. Korevaar, E.J., et al.: Status of sdio/is&t lasercom testbed program. In: Free-Space Laser Communication Technologies V, vol. 1866, pp. 116–127. SPIE (1993)
15. Kumar, N.P., Jatoth, R.K.: Development of cloud based light intensity monitoring system using raspberry pi. In: 2015 International Conference on Industrial Instrumentation and Control (ICIC), pp. 1356–1361. IEEE (2015)

16. Leens, F.: An introduction to i 2 c and spi protocols. IEEE Instrum. Measur. Mag. **12**(1), 8–13 (2009)
17. Li, Y.G., Stuber, G.L.: Orthogonal frequency division multiplexing for wireless communications. Springer Science & Business Media (2006)
18. Liu, M.: Design and implementation of smart home system based on stm32. In: 2022 4th International Academic Exchange Conference on Science and Technology Innovation (IAECST), pp. 1352–1357. IEEE (2022)
19. Madhow, U., Honig, M.L.: Mmse interference suppression for direct-sequence spread-spectrum cdma. IEEE Trans. Commun. **42**(12), 3178–3188 (1994)
20. Niu, Y., Zhou, L., Liu, Z.: A deep looking at the code changes in openharmony. In: Asia-Pacific Web (APWeb) and Web-Age Information Management (WAIM) Joint International Conference on Web and Big Data, pp. 426–434. Springer, Cham (2022). https://doi.org/10.1007/978-3-031-25158-0_34
21. Norhuzaimin, J., Maimun, H.: The design of high speed uart. In: 2005 Asia-Pacific Conference on Applied Electromagnetics, pp. 5-pp. IEEE (2005)
22. Nugraha, A.T., As' ad, R.F., Abdullayev, V.H., et al.: Design and fabrication of temperature and humidity stabilizer on low voltage distribution panel with plc-based fuzzy method to prevent excessive temperature and humidity on the panel. J. Electron. Electromed. Eng. Med. Inform. **4**(3), 170–177 (2022)
23. Pierleoni, P., Concetti, R., Belli, A., Palma, L.: Amazon, google and microsoft solutions for iot: architectures and a performance comparison. IEEE Access **8**, 5455–5470 (2019)
24. Roland, M., Langer, J.: Digital signature records for the nfc data exchange format. In: 2010 Second International Workshop on Near Field Communication, pp. 71–76. IEEE (2010)
25. Roy, A., Das, P., Das, R.: Temperature and humidity monitoring system for storage rooms of industries. In: 2017 International Conference on Computing and Communication Technologies for Smart Nation (IC3TSN), pp. 99–103. IEEE (2017)
26. Wang, X.: Analysis of thread schedulability in huawei liteos. In: MATEC Web of Conferences, vol. 336, p. 05031. EDP Sciences (2021)
27. Want, R.: Near field communication. IEEE Pervasive Comput. **10**(3), 4–7 (2011)
28. Waterman, A.S.: Design of the RISC-V instruction set architecture. University of California, Berkeley (2016)
29. Xiao, J., Li, J.T.: Design and implementation of intelligent temperature and humidity monitoring system based on zigbee and wifi. Procedia Comput. Sci. **166**, 419–422 (2020)
30. Zhang, H., Chen, S., Zou, P., Xiong, G., Zhao, H., Zhang, Y.: Research and application of industrial equipment management service system based on cloud-edge collaboration. In: 2019 Chinese Automation Congress (CAC), pp. 5451–5456 (2019). https://doi.org/10.1109/CAC48633.2019.8996876
31. Zhang, L.: Iot and fusion algorithm based agriculture system. In: International Conference on Internet of Things and Machine Learning (IoTML 2022), vol. 12640, pp. 30–34. SPIE (2023)

YOLO-IMF: An Improved YOLOv8 Algorithm for Surface Defect Detection in Industrial Manufacturing Field

Ziqiang Liu[1,2] and Kejiang Ye[1(✉)]

[1] Shenzhen Institute of Advanced Technology, Chinese Academy of Sciences,
Shenzhen 518055, China
{zq.liu6,kj.ye}@siat.ac.cn
[2] University of Science and Technology of China, Hefei 230026, China

Abstract. Surface quality is an effective metric to evaluate the quality of industrial products. The traditional automatic detection methods such as eddy current detection method, infrared detection method and magnetic flux leakage method are limited to particular environments and cannot achieve satisfied accuracy. Deep learning based vision detection such as YOLO algorithm is a new promising method. However, due to complex real industrial environment, the direct use of existing methods still has some limitations. To solve the challenge, in this paper, we propose an improved YOLOv8 algorithm - YOLO-IMF to address the issue of surface defect recognition on aluminum plates. By replacing the CIOU loss function with the EIOU loss function, we can better measure the similarity between small targets and targets with irregular shapes, thereby enhancing the effectiveness of bounding box regression. Experimental results demonstrate an obvious improvement in defect detection, with a mean precision increasing from 98.1% to 99.3%. Moreover, the detection performance outperforms YOLOv5m and Faster R-CNN algorithms.

Keywords: Surface defect detection · YOLOv8 · Industrial manufacturing · Product quality

1 Introduction

Product quality is the core goal pursued by modern industry. However, in real industrial environment, the product quality may affected by many factors. Surface quality is an effective metric to evaluate the quality of industrial products. Taking aluminum sheet manufacturing industry as an example, the surface of the aluminum sheet will produce defects such as wrinkles, dirt, pinholes and scraps due to the influence of various factors such as production processes. These defects will seriously affect the quality of the aluminum sheet.

To improve the product quality, machine-automated defect detection on the product surface becomes very important [1]. In the early days, the defect detection of industrial products was mainly observed by human eyes, which had high

© The Author(s), under exclusive license to Springer Nature Switzerland AG 2023
S. He et al. (Eds.): METAVERSE 2023, LNCS 14210, pp. 15–28, 2023.
https://doi.org/10.1007/978-3-031-44754-9_2

requirements on the ability of inspectors and the detection was greatly affected by subjective factors.

Automatic detection has become an inevitable choice [2]. The commonly used defect detection methods include eddy current detection method, infrared detection method, magnetic flux leakage method and machine vision based detection method [3]. The first three methods are not widely used due to the limitations of their detection principles. For a wide variety of defects, the detection accuracy cannot reach a satisfactory level. While the fourth detection method based on machine vision has gradually replaced the first three. This method is widely used in the field of industrial non-destructive testing, which benefits from the rapid development of today's Charge-Coupled Device (CCD) technology, laser technology and computer technology.

But most of the machine vision methods use common image processing technology to extract features and detect defects. New descriptions of defects can also be made from different angles, such as areas surrounded by edges, areas with uneven texture and areas that are uneven and bumpy. According to these characteristics, new detection methods such as edge-based defect detection methods, texture-based defect detection methods, and defect detection methods based on unevenness are proposed to improve the detection efficiency.

In recent years, deep learning has been widely used in the field of image detection and recognition. For example, convolutional neural network are usually used for surface defect detection [4]. At present, there are two mainstream methods for deep learning of object detection tasks: i) Two-stage method: obtain some anchor boxes first, and then classify and return the result, such as Fast R-CNN, Faster R- CNN, etc.; ii) One-stage method: also known as end-to-end detection method, such as YOLO, SSD, etc. The two-stage method has high accuracy, but the detection speed is slow; while the one-stage method is not as accurate as the first one, but the detection speed is faster. These object detection methods are all based on deep convolutional networks.

To overcome the limits of the existing methods, in this paper, we focus on a practical problem of aluminum sheet defect detection and develop a new surface defect detection method - YOLO-IMF which is extended from the recent YOLOv8 objective detection algorithm [5]. The contributions of this paper is summarized as follows:

- We propose a new defect detection algorithm - YOLO-IMF to detect the product surface defects (i.e. aluminum defects), then further improve the loss function based on YOLOv8 to improve the detection effect of small defects in aluminum sheets.
- We conduct experimental verification on an aluminum sheet data set. The experimental results show that mAP (mean Average Precision) of the improved algorithm is 1.2% higher than YOLOv8.

The reminder of this paper is organized as follows: In Sect. 2, we present the related work of object detection. The proposed method is introduced in Sect. 3. Section 4 introduces the dataset. Section 5 is the experiment, in which we introduce the evaluation metrics and the results. Finally the conclusions are given in Sect. 6.

2   Related Work

Object detection is one of the most basic tasks in the field of computer vision and is usually used for defect detection. The purpose is to obtain accurate location and category information of the object. At present, object detection methods based on deep learning develop very fast. Generally speaking, the defect detection network based on deep learning can be divided into Two-stage network represented by Faster R-CNN (Region-CNN) [6], and One-stage network represented by SSD (Single shout multibax detector) [7] or YOLO (You only look once) [8]. The main difference between the two networks is that the two-stage network needs to first generate a proposal that may contain defects, and then proceed to object detection. While the one-stage network directly uses the features extracted in the network to predict the location and category of defects.

2.1   Two-Stage Detection Network

Faster R-CNN (Region Convolutional Neural Network) is an advanced and popular object detection algorithm that was developed as an improvement over previous models like R-CNN and Fast R-CNN.

At its core, Faster R-CNN operates in two stages. In the first stage, it uses a Region Proposal Network (RPN) to generate region proposals, which are areas that might contain an object. The RPN is fully convolutional, which means it can handle input images of any size. This first stage acts as an attention mechanism, directing the model towards regions of the image that are most likely to contain an object.

In the second stage, the algorithm performs classification and bounding box regression on these region proposals, ultimately detecting the objects within these regions and accurately locating them in the image. This is done by extracting features using a Region of Interest (RoI) pooling layer, which warps the region proposals into a fixed size so they can be processed by a fully connected layer.

In 2020, Tao et al. [9] designed a two-stage Faster R-CNN network for the location of insulator defects in unmanned aerial vehicle (UAV) power line inspections. The first stage is designed for locating insulator regions in natural scenes, while the second stage focuses on defect localization within the identified insulator regions. Xue et al. [10] developed an improved Faster R-CNN model for defect detection in shield tunneling. They employed an enhanced Inception fully convolutional network as the Backbone to obtain feature maps. Additionally, they introduced two additional anchor box ratios and utilized position-sensitive ROIpooling instead of the traditional ROIpooling. The proposed model achieved a detection accuracy of over 95% with a testing time speed of 48ms per image. The detection method using Faster R-CNN is also widely used in defect detection fields such as tunnels [11], liquid crystal panel polarizer surfaces [12], thermal imaging insulator defects [13], aluminum profile surfaces [14] and tire hubs [15].

2.2   One-Stage Detection Network

There are two types of one-stage detection networks: SSD and YOLO, both of which use the entire image as the input of the network directly regresses the location of the bounding box and the category it belongs to at the output layer. The feature of SSD is that it introduces a feature pyramid detection method to predict the target position and category from feature maps of different scales. It uses 6 different feature maps to detect objects of different scales.

YOLOv5, which stands for "You Only Look Once version 5", is an advanced object detection algorithm known for its speed and efficiency. YOLOv5 maintains the "single pass detection" philosophy of the YOLO series and brings in several enhancements. It provides versatile model scaling to cater to different computational needs and precision requirements, introduces advanced data augmentation techniques to boost the model's robustness, and optimizes the balance between speed and detection performance. Its design also focuses on user-friendliness, supporting easy deployment with features like auto-download of weights and simple conversion to formats like ONNX or TorchScript. These attributes have made YOLOv5 a popular choice in real-time object detection applications such as autonomous driving, surveillance, and robotics.

Chen et al. [16] used the improved SSD network to locate the fastener defect area on the catenary support device, and the main improvement part is to use the feature maps of different layers for target detection. Li et al. [17] proposed a detection method for container sealing surface defects in the filling production line based on MobileNet-SSD, and optimized the Backbone structure of SSD through MobileNet to simplify the detection model parameters.

Liu et al. [18] also used the MobileNet-SSD network to locate the supporting components of the high-speed railway catenary. Compared with the original SSD network, the improvements are as follows: using MobileNet as the Backbone; only using 4 different feature maps to speed up object detection. On the tested dataset, its goal achieves a detection speed of 25 frames/s and a mAP of 94.3%. Meng et al. [19] proposed a solar cell defect detection method based on the improved YOLOv5 algorithm in view of the complex background of solar cell images, variable defect shapes, and large differences. Compared with the original YOLOv5 network, mosaic and mixed Integrate data augmentation, K-means++ clustering anchor box algorithm and CIOU loss function to improve model performance.

3   YOLO-IMF Algorithm

3.1   YOLOv8

YOLOv8 is a SOTA model [5] that builds on the success of previous YOLO versions, and introduces new features and improvements to further improve performance and flexibility. Specific innovations include a new backbone network, a new Ancher-Free detection head, and a new loss function that can run on a variety of hardware platforms from CPUs to GPUs. The new SOTA model includes a P5 640 and P6 1280 resolution object detection network and a YOLACT-based instance segmentation model. Like YOLOv5, different size models of N/S/M/L/X scales are also provided based on the scaling factor to meet the needs of different scenarios.

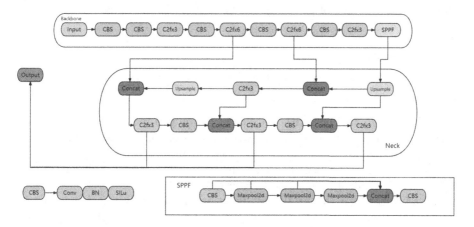

Fig. 1. The network structure of YOLOv8.

The backbone network and Neck part may refer to the design idea of YOLOv7 ELAN. The C3 structure of YOLOv5 is replaced by the C2f structure with richer gradient flow, and different channel numbers are adjusted for different scale models. It is a brainless set of parameters applied to all models, which greatly improves the performance of the model. However, operations such as Split in this C2f module are not as friendly to specific hardware deployment as before.

Compared with YOLOv5, the Head part has changed a lot, replacing it with the current mainstream decoupling head structure, separating the classification and detection heads, and also changing from Anchor-Based to Anchor-Free.

In terms of Loss calculation, the TaskAlignedAssigner positive sample allocation strategy is adopted, and Distribution Focal Loss is introduced.

The data enhancement part of the training introduces the last 10 epoch in YOLOX to turn off the Mosiac enhancement operation, which can effectively improve the accuracy. Figure 1 depicts the network structure of YOLOv8.

3.2   ELOU

Although CIOU Loss considers the overlapping area, center point distance, and aspect ratio of the bounding box regression. However, the difference in the aspect ratio reflected by v (measuring the similarity of aspect ratios) in its formula is not the real difference between the width and height and their confidence, so sometimes it will hinder the model from effectively optimizing the similarity. Zhang et al. [20] disassembled the aspect ratio on the basis of CIOU, proposed

EIOU Loss, and added Focal to focus on high-quality anchor frames. The EIou loss function can be seen as adding two additional penalty items on the basis of the traditional IoU indicator: the Euclidean distance penalty item and the angle difference penalty item. The Euclidean distance penalty can make the center point of the predicted bounding box and the real bounding box closer, thereby improving the accuracy of positioning. The formula for EIOU is:

$$\ell_{EIoU} = \ell_{IoU} + \ell_{dis} + \ell_{asp}$$
$$= 1 - IoU + \frac{\rho^2 (b, b^{gt})}{c^2} + \frac{\rho^2 (w, w^{gt})}{C_w^2} + \frac{\rho^2 (h, h^{gt})}{C_h^2} \tag{1}$$

where C_w and C_h are the width and height of the two rectangles, respectively. It can be seen from this that EIOU divides the loss function into three parts, IOU loss, distance loss, and edge length loss. It can be seen that EIOU directly uses the side length as a penalty item, which can also solve the problem of side length being magnified by mistake to a certain extent.

The advantages of the EIOU loss function are as follows: i) It can better measure the similarity between small objects and irregularly shaped objects, thereby improving the effect of bounding box regression. ii) It can be compatible with different bounding box representations, such as center point coordinates, width and height, angle, etc., thereby improving the versatility and flexibility of the algorithm. iii) It can effectively avoid some common bounding box regression problems, such as zero gradient, local optimum, etc., thereby improving the stability and convergence of the algorithm.

4   Dataset

Figure 2 shows an example of surface defect images of aluminum sheets used for training and evaluation, each image has a resolution of 640×480 pixels. The aluminum sheet surface defect data set comes from an aluminum company. The data set of industrial defect detection on the surface of aluminum sheets is collected by Hikvision industrial cameras. The data set is marked in COCO format, which contains four categories of defect targets: pinholes, dirt, wrinkles, and scratches. The data set has more than 1400 labeled pictures. In order to obtain the training data set, images are randomly selected from the entire data set. The training data set contains 70% of the images. Therefore, there are 980 images for training, 140 images for evaluation, and 280 images for testing. We use random functions to partition the dataset, ensuring that the test set has the same data distribution as the complete dataset. It includes a variety of examples to ensure that the model's performance can be measured in as many possible scenarios as possible. Figure 3 shows the characteristics of the annotated defect in the training set. These four charts illustrate key features and distributions within the training data, playing a crucial role in understanding the data and making appropriate model selections and optimizations:

Figure 3(a) (Training set data volume): This chart shows the number of defects in each category, which is crucial for understanding the class balance within the dataset. If some classes have significantly more samples than others, strategies might need to be deployed to handle class imbalance, such as over-sampling minority classes, under-sampling majority classes, or using class weights.

Figure 3(b) (Bounding box size and count): This chart shows the annotation boxes in the training set. This information is essential for setting model parameters (such as anchor sizes in object detection models) and preprocessing the data (such as scaling or cropping images).

Figure 3(c) (Center point relative to the entire image): This chart shows the position of the centroid relative to the entire image. It helps to understand if there's any pattern in the spatial distribution of objects or if objects tend to appear at certain locations in the images.

Figure 3(d) (Target aspect ratio relative to the entire image): This chart shows the aspect ratio of the object relative to the entire image. If the shape of objects varies significantly, this might need to be taken into account to improve our model or preprocessing steps.

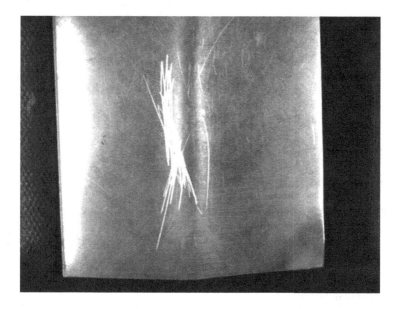

Fig. 2. An example of defective image of aluminum sheets.

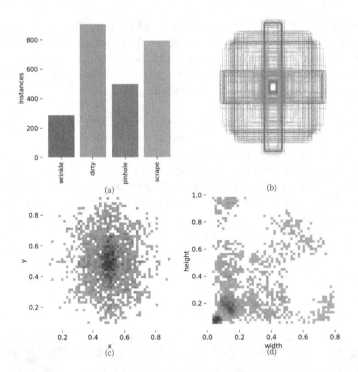

Fig. 3. The defective labels: (a) shows the number of defects in each category; (b) shows the annotation boxes in the training set; (c) shows the position of the centroid relative to the entire image and (d) shows the aspect ratio of the object relative to the entire image.

5   Experiments

5.1   Experimental Platform

The operating system used for the experiments in this paper is Ubuntu 22.04, and the system hardware facilities are 32G RAM, NVIDIA GTX3080 GPU, and Intel(R) Xeon(R) Platinum 8255C CPU. The software platform used is torch 2.0.1 + cuda11.7 and Anaconda.

5.2   Valuation Index

The valuation index included mean average precision (mAP), average precision (AP), precision (P), and recall (R). The formulas for P and R are defined in Eqs. (2) and (3).

$$P = \frac{TP}{(TP + FP)} \tag{2}$$

$$R = \frac{TP}{(TP + FN)} \tag{3}$$

TP is the number of correctly predicted bounding boxes, FP is the number of incorrectly judged positive samples, and FN is the number of undetected targets. AP is the average accuracy of the model. mAP is the average value of the AP. k is the number of categories. The formulas for AP and mAP are as shown in Eqs. (4) and (5).

$$AP = \int_0^1 p(r)dr \tag{4}$$

$$mAP = \frac{1}{k} \sum_{i=1}^{k} AP_i \tag{5}$$

5.3 Experimental Result

We use YOLOv8 as a benchmark model to compare with the improved model YOLO-IMF. YOLO-IMF replaces the CIOU loss function in YOLOv8 with the EIOU loss function to improve the positioning accuracy of the target box. We use the same network structure, hyperparameters and training strategy, but change the loss function. The AdamW optimizer is used for training, the learning rate is set to 0.01, the batchsize is 128, and the number of training epochs is set to 100. Figure 4 and Fig. 5 compares the loss and mAP during the training process. Figure 4 shows that the loss of YOLO-IMF decreases faster than that of YOLOv8. Figure 5 shows that the mAP@0.5 of YOLO-IMF is higher than that of YOLOv8. A higher mAP value indicates that the object detection model performs better on the given dataset.

Figure 6 shows the experimental results of the two models on the test set. Our proposed improved model YOLO-IMF outperforms the baseline model by 1.2% in mAP for both individual classes and all classes. This shows that the improved model can better locate and identify the defects on the aluminum sheet and improve the detection quality.

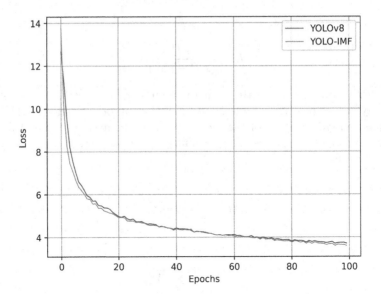

Fig. 4. Loss comparison chart during training.

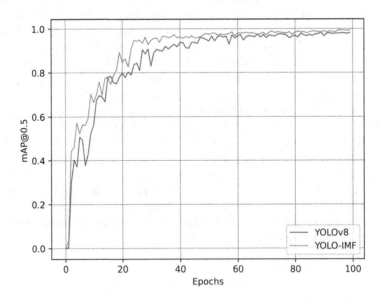

Fig. 5. mAP@0.5 comparison chart during training.

The performance comparison of common object detection algorithms and the improved YOLOv8 algorithm on the aluminum plate defect dataset is shown in Table 1. It can be observed that in terms of detection accuracy, the algorithm proposed in this paper has improved the YOLOv8 algorithm and the Faster R-CNN algorithm by 1.2% and 6.9% respectively.

The detection results of the improved YOLOv8 algorithm for defects detection are shown in Fig. 7.

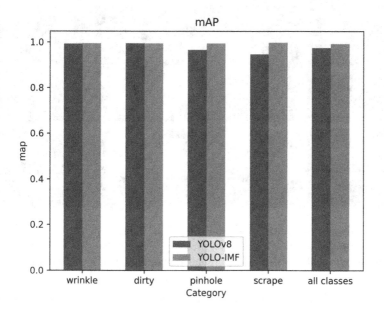

Fig. 6. All classes mAP comparison chart during testing.

Table 1. Performance composition with other methods.

Model	mAP@0.5
Faster R-CNN	92.4%
YOLOv5m	97.7%
YOLOv6m	97.5%
YOLOv8m	98.1%
YOLO-IMF	**99.3%**

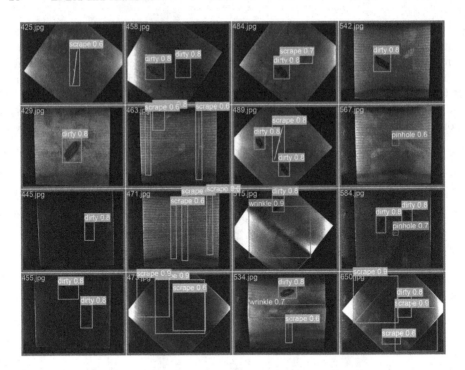

Fig. 7. The prediction result of YOLO-IMF. The number in different color represents the prediction likelihood. Yellows represents scrape defect, red represents wrinkle defect, pink represents dirty defect, orange represents pinhole defect. (Color figure online)

6   Conclusion

In response to the limitations of the original YOLOv8 algorithm in surface defect detection on aluminum plates, we propose a new improved algorithm - YOLO-IMF, by optimizing the loss function. The EIOU provides faster convergence speed and resolves the issue of incorrect enlargement of side lengths. Experimental results demonstrate a certain degree of enhancement in defect detection, with a mean precision increasing from 98.1% to 99.3%. Furthermore, the detection performance surpasses that of YOLOv5m and Faster R-CNN algorithms. Through the experiments, we conclude that YOLO-IMF achieves efficient detection of surface defects on aluminum plates, offering a new direction for intelligent metal quality inspection.

Acknowledgment. This work is supported by the National Key R&D Program of China (No. 2021YFB3300200), National Natural Science Foundation of China (No. 92267105), Guangdong Special Support Plan (No. 2021TQ06X990), Shenzhen Basic Research Program (No. JCYJ20200109115418592, JCYJ20220818101610023).

References

1. Parlak, I.E., Emel, E.: Deep learning-based detection of aluminum casting defects and their types. Eng. Appl. Artif. Intell. **118**, 105636 (2023)
2. Sun, X., Jinan, G., Tang, S., Li, J.: Research progress of visual inspection technology of steel products-a review. Appl. Sci. **8**(11), 2195 (2018)
3. Shi, Y., Zhang, C., Li, R., Cai, M., Jia, G.: Theory and application of magnetic flux leakage pipeline detection. Sensors **15**(12), 31036–31055 (2015)
4. Mery, D.: Aluminum casting inspection using deep learning: a method based on convolutional neural networks. J. Nondestr. Eval. **39**(1), 12 (2020)
5. Jocher, G., Chaurasia, A., Qiu, J.: Ultralytics yolov8 (2023)
6. Ren, S., He, K., Girshick, R., Sun, J.: Faster R-CNN: towards real-time object detection with region proposal networks. In: Advances in Neural Information Processing Systems, 28 (2015)
7. Liu, W., Anguelov, D., Erhan, D., Szegedy, C., Reed, S., Fu, C.-Y., Berg, A.C.: SSD: single shot MultiBox detector. In: Leibe, B., Matas, J., Sebe, N., Welling, M. (eds.) ECCV 2016. LNCS, vol. 9905, pp. 21–37. Springer, Cham (2016). https://doi.org/10.1007/978-3-319-46448-0_2
8. Redmon, J., Divvala, S., Girshick, R., Farhadi, A.: You only look once: unified, real-time object detection. In: Proceedings of the IEEE Conference on Computer Vision and Pattern Recognition, pp. 779–788 (2016)
9. Tao, X., Zhang, D., Wang, Z., Liu, X., Zhang, H., De, X.: Detection of power line insulator defects using aerial images analyzed with convolutional neural networks. IEEE Trans. Syst. Man Cybern. Syst. **50**(4), 1486–1498 (2018)
10. Xue, Y., Li, Y.: A fast detection method via region-based fully convolutional neural networks for shield tunnel lining defects. Comput.-Aided Civil Infrastruct. Eng. **33**(8), 638–654 (2018)
11. Cheng, J.C.P., Wang, M.: Automated detection of sewer pipe defects in closed-circuit television images using deep learning techniques. Autom. Constr. **95**, 155–171 (2018)
12. Lei, H., Wang, B., Hehe, W., Wang, A.: Defect detection for polymeric polarizer based on faster r-cnn. J. Inf. Hiding Multim. Signal Process. **9**(6), 1414–1420 (2018)
13. Zhao, Z., Zhen, Z., Zhang, L., Qi, Y., Kong, Y., Zhang, K.: Insulator detection method in inspection image based on improved faster R-CNN. Energies **12**(7), 1204 (2019)
14. Neuhauser, F.M., Bachmann, G., Hora, P.: Surface defect classification and detection on extruded aluminum profiles using convolutional neural networks. Int. J. Mater. Forming **13**, 591–603 (2020)
15. Sun, X., Jinan, G., Huang, R., Zou, R., Palomares, B.G.: Surface defects recognition of wheel hub based on improved faster R-CNN. Electronics **8**(5), 481 (2019)
16. Chen, J., Liu, Z., Wang, H., Núñez, A., Han, Z.: Automatic defect detection of fasteners on the catenary support device using deep convolutional neural network. IEEE Trans. Instrum. Meas. **67**(2), 257–269 (2017)
17. Li, Y., Huang, H., Xie, Q., Yao, L., Chen, Q.: Research on a surface defect detection algorithm based on mobilenet-ssd. Appl. Sci. **8**(9), 1678 (2018)
18. Liu, Z., Liu, K., Zhong, J., Han, Z., Zhang, W.: A high-precision positioning approach for catenary support components with multiscale difference. IEEE Trans. Instrum. Meas. **69**(3), 700–711 (2019)

19. Zhang, M., Yin, L.: Solar cell surface defect detection based on improved yolo v5. IEEE Access **10**, 80804–80815 (2022)
20. Zhang, Y.-F., Ren, W., Zhang, Z., Jia, Z., Wang, L., Tan, T.: Focal and efficient IOU loss for accurate bounding box regression. Neurocomputing **506**, 146–157 (2022)

The Path Analysis of Applying VR Technology to University Ideological and Political Theory Courses

Cunling Liu and Wei Tang[✉]

Shenzhen Institute of Information Technology, Guangdong 518172, People's Republic of China
123938125@qq.com

Abstract. With the rapid development of information technology, the influence of "integrating media" on college students is both a challenge and an opportunity. As one of the important compulsory courses for college students, ideological and political theory courses need to be constantly updated with the new teaching methods. VR technology is a new application technology with unique advantages, therefore, integrating VR technology into the classroom of college students can effectively narrow the distance with college students, so that the teaching content can be implanted in the hearts of students. The embedding of VR virtual simulation technology in the education and teaching of ideological and political courses has effectively enhanced the identity of contemporary college students to the country and enhanced their learning of theoretical cognition.

Keywords: financial media · VR technology · Ideological and political education · Immersive experience

1 Introduction

As of June 2023, China's Internet penetration rate has reached 75.6%, of which 99.6% use mobile phones to access the Internet, according to the China Industry Information Network. The rapid development of the Internet has led to the rapid development of "financial media", and new technologies and media have long penetrated into most people's lives and work, becoming an indispensable part. The influence of new technology and new media on contemporary college students is also obvious. "Network learning" has become an important way for contemporary college students to acquire knowledge, and long-term network learning has affected their learning style. In other words, with the rapid development of information technology and Internet technology, people's study, work and life are more and more integrated into the "Internet+" model, and college students are no exception. The "Internet + ideological and political course" model has gradually become a new tool to carry out ideological and political education in colleges and universities. On the one hand, it enriches and broadens the teaching resources of ideological and political courses in colleges and universities. On the other hand, it also brings certain possibilities to the innovation of ideological and political course teaching. (As shown in Fig. 1).

S. He et al. (Eds.): METAVERSE 2023, LNCS 14210, pp. 29–38, 2023.
https://doi.org/10.1007/978-3-031-44754-9_3

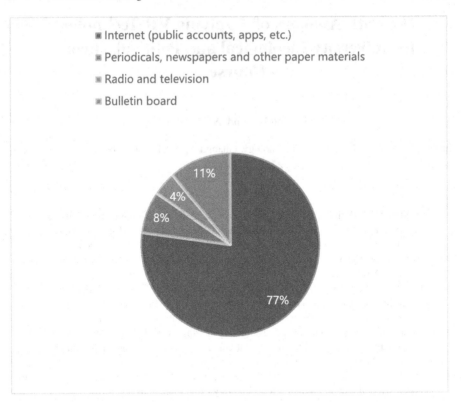

Fig. 1.

According to the survey, as shown in Fig. 1, 77% of students said that they would acquire knowledge related to ideological and political courses through the Internet and 11% through the public publicity column. From the survey results, it can be seen that the Internet has undoubtedly become the main channel for college students to acquire ideological and political knowledge. Under the background of "Internet+", colleges and universities can transcend the boundaries of time and space, share excellent courses of ideological and political courses, set collective wisdom in one, jointly explore frontier issues of disciplines, and promote the development of disciplines. Compared with traditional media, the Internet has unique advantages. It integrates sound, picture, text and film and television into one, turning the sampling into concrete and static into dynamic, effectively alleviating the boredom of traditional teaching classrooms and breaking traditional limitations. In short, the development of Internet technology has narrowed the distance between college students and ideological and political courses, and realized the complementary advantage of resources.

It is not difficult to find from the above survey that under the background of new media and new technology, it is one of the problems to be solved to strengthen and improve the ideological and political education of college students, let the ideological and political education enter the hearts of students, arouse the resonance of students and get the recognition of students. Virtual Reality technology, referred to as VR technology, realizes the organic interaction between real scenes and virtual space within a certain range through human-computer interaction, and guides experients to immerse themselves in the "realistic" environment of virtual simulation in terms of sight, sound and touch, so as to obtain "real" feelings and experiences. In the ideological and political class, students experience red cultural resources and real historical scenes in a real-time interactive way by manipulating external devices connected in virtual space. Through VR technology, the real scenes of the class content in the classroom are presented to students through virtual simulation technology, so that students can truly feel those shocking and educational scenes, which can make students have a great shock, so as to achieve good situational teaching effect. However, at present, there are still some problems affecting the practical teaching effectiveness of ideological and political courses, such as teachers' indoctrination in class, students' passive acceptance of content, the lack of effective teaching and learning interaction between teachers and students, and the lack of practical teaching resources.

2 The Realistic Dilemma of the Education and Teaching of Ideological and Political Theory Courses in Universities

2.1 Teachers' Teaching Content is Too Theoretical

When teaching courses, some teachers are too rigid in teaching content, not according to the law of students' growth and development, creative use of teaching materials, combined with students' actual needs and interest points to generate diversified teaching content. Ideological and political teaching content is the information link between teachers and students. When asked "What problems do you think exist in the current teaching content of ideological and political theory courses", 68% of students think that the teaching content of ideological and political courses is "theoretical and boring", 72% of students think that the teaching content is "lack of vitality", and 71% of students think that "the content is less suitable for students' reality". Sixty-three percent of students found teaching cases too old to resonate. To a certain extent, these statistics can reflect that the teaching content of ideological and political courses in some universities is still too theoretical, and does not pay attention to the actual needs of students for the teaching content, which is not suitable for the actual life of students, and the teaching form does not effectively integrate the use of information technology (as shown in Fig. 2).

A good teaching design means that the more students interact effectively, the better the classroom effect will be. If the important and difficult points of the teaching design are not prominent and the details are not appropriate, the integrity, coherence and logic of the teaching content will be reduced, and of course, it will be unattractive. However, it does not mean that teachers should blindly cater to students' "tastes". On the one hand, teachers should have a thorough understanding of the teaching materials, on the other hand, they should rely on the teaching materials, and use targeted teaching design and teaching methods to improve the attractiveness of the teaching content for students with different majors and different educational backgrounds, so as to impart the teaching content comprehensively and specifically to students.

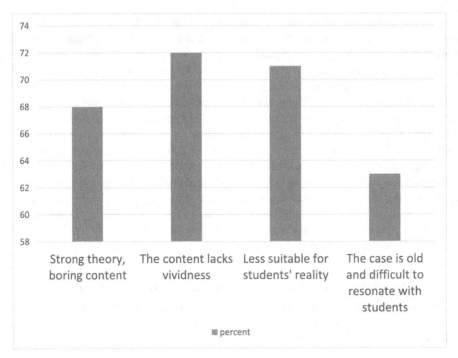

Fig. 2.

2.2 Teachers' Teaching Concepts are Outdated and Lacking in Appeal

Teaching methods play an important role in ideological and political teaching. Effective, appropriate and appropriate teaching methods can enable educators to deliver teaching content to educational objects better and accomplish educational goals efficiently and quickly. To improve the teaching methods of ideological and political courses, so that students are willing to accept and easy to understand, is an important factor for students to master the teaching content. Aiming at what kind of ideological and political teaching methods college students like in the new era, this paper makes statistics on relevant data and draws the following results: (as shown in Fig. 3)

As can be seen from the above figure, practical teaching method and heuristic teaching method are the most popular among students, while classroom teaching method, situational teaching method and debate and discussion method, as supplementary teaching methods, can bring stronger attraction and interest to the course. Among them, the traditional classroom teaching method accounted for 65.3%, which can be seen that the traditional teaching method has an irreplaceable role in the teaching method of ideological and political courses. However, in order to make the ideological and political courses more friendly, it is necessary to coordinate the use of various teaching methods and avoid the single use of methods. In the process of classroom teaching, some ideological and political teachers have a single teaching method, which leads to a depressed classroom atmosphere, less interaction between teachers and students, and weak emotional resonance. In addition, when asked how students hope to improve the affinity of ideological

Item	NUMBER OF PEOPLE	PERCENT（%）
PRACTICAL TEACHING METHOD	693	76.6
HEURISTIC TEACHING METHOD	668	73.4
CLASSROOM TEACHING METHOD	590	65.3
SITUATIONAL DEDUCTION METHOD	584	64.6
ARGUMENTATIVE METHOD	468	51.8

Fig. 3. College Students' Preference for Ideological and Political Teaching Methods (Multiple Choices)

and political education in colleges and universities, some college students proposed that they hope to increase more course-related practical activities to enhance students' sense of participation and experience, which also reflects the need to optimize practical content and activities to make students have a sense of gain. As a bridge between the educator and the object of education, the educational method itself plays a role of communication and connection, so once the educational method lacks effective interaction and participation, it will lose its affinity. If teachers use the classroom teaching method too much, and it is difficult to integrate practical teaching method and heuristic teaching method into the classroom, it will lead to the lack of appeal of teachers, difficult to attract students' attention, difficult to mobilize students' enthusiasm for learning, and ultimately difficult to win students' love, and lack of curriculum affinity.

2.3 Lack of Teaching Resources and Unreasonable Use of New Technology and Media

Although many teachers have adopted new media technologies, there are still many limitations in their actual use. Most of them simply use short video platforms or pictures for display, and it is difficult for a single output carrier to be in a passive state of learning. Traditional teaching forms interaction with students, while contemporary college students prefer to use new technologies and media for real-time interaction, so it is difficult for short video platforms or picture displays to arouse students' learning interest. In addition, some colleges and universities have insufficient investment in curriculum education and teaching resources, and the uneven distribution of resources is also one of the important reasons that hinder the practical teaching of this course.

3 VR Technology Plays an Important Role in the Teaching of Ideological and Political Theory Courses in Universities

As a new media technology, VR technology has unique advantages, which can simulate virtual scenes through computers, visualize relevant content, and give the experiencer the feeling of "immersive". Strong sense of immersive experience and human-computer interaction is one of the advantages of VR virtual simulation. Under the background of "fusion media", VR technology is embedded in practical teaching of ideological and political courses, and historical scenes and red cultural resources are visualized in front of students to maximize the expansion of teaching space. Enhancing college students' interest in ideological and political courses can stimulate college students' interest in learning and expand their thinking ability, improve their sense of involvement in teaching situations and enhance authenticity, break through the limitations of time and space, and improve participation, thus guiding students to transform from passive education to active exploration (as shown in Fig. 4).

Fig. 4. Highlights the design method of students' Subjectivity

3.1   Is Conducive to Stimulating College Students' Interest in Learning and Expanding Their Thinking Ability

Under the new technology, college students widely use various we-media platforms such as wechat and Douyin, which are highly innovative and attractive. However, in the era of value diversification, long-term use of the we-media platform will affect college students to establish correct values. The "immersive" experience based on VR virtual simulation can strengthen the interaction between inside and outside the school, narrow the distance with college students, and make the course content more interesting. With the help of VR virtual simulation, using its unique technical characteristics and attributes, to create a new ideological and political education teaching method, which can stimulate the interest of college students. As one of the "integrated media" technologies, 3D three-dimensional presentation is the biggest advantage brought by VR technology. VR technology into the classroom teaching, a good visualization of some of the more complex theories, and with the inherent Internet thinking. The creative use of VR technology to teach college students not only increases their appeal, but also enhances the learning effect. The integration of VR technology avoids the mode of simple teacher teaching and students listening to lectures, and more importantly, it guides students to have immersive experience while learning. Through the human-computer interaction of VR technology, the "communication" between college students and the delivered content is enhanced, and college students are guided to resonate.

At the same time, "VR + teaching resources" is a powerful starting point to improve the effectiveness of ideological and political education for college students. The teaching content is organically combined with various teaching resources, and VR technology is used to simulate "real scenes" to guide students to immersive experience, avoid monotonous teaching, stimulate their learning interest, and expand their learning thinking ability. In the teaching, with the help of VR technology platform, the Chinese story is told in a visual and interactive way, which can present the real history in front of students, and help the ideological and political course to be truly "fresh" from the content to the form, and enhance the teaching effect. VR technology can effectively extend the teaching form of ideological and political courses in colleges and universities, stimulate students to change from "passive acceptance" to "active exploration", and truly make students become the main body of the classroom and truly participate in teaching with teachers. The sharing and interactive advantages of VR technology can help students better understand abstract theories. Teachers can set open questions and virtual simulation scenes according to the teaching content, and guide students to think about related issues in a relaxed and immersive environment. Guide students to learn new knowledge through active learning, stimulate their subjective initiative in learning through experience, and cultivate their thinking and ability to explore true knowledge. Therefore, VR technology is embedded in the university classroom, and the relevant content of the course is displayed in a three-dimensional manner in front of the students through the fresh media that they are happy to see and accept, which enhances the effectiveness, pertinence and interest of education and teaching, and releases the vitality of education.

3.2 VR Technology is Conducive to Improving the Sense of Immersion in Teaching Situations

VR technology builds a bridge between "real existence" and "virtual simulation", so that the "virtual" and "real" can be effectively connected. In the teaching process, teachers can better grasp the dynamics of students' thoughts and their development laws by understanding the real ideas of students. In other words, teachers can consider the issues they are concerned about from the perspective of students and start from the students themselves, and can better promote the teaching content into the brain. As a new type of teaching practice, VR technology still follows the material production practice advocated by Marxist practice view. With the rapid development of VR technology, the practical teaching mode of ideological and political course has been deepened. The organic integration of "VR technology + teaching resources" into teaching is an organic combination of "theory" and "practice". This "practice" can be a fresh story or a memorable revolutionary story. Through VR technology, history can be repeated, improving the sense of teaching situation and enhancing students' sense of experience. VR technology is embedded in practical teaching in colleges and universities, allowing college students to experience different ideological and political education outside the traditional classroom. Students are in a "real" environment where immersive, interactive, perceptive and intelligent experiences not only stimulate interest in learning, but also increase engagement.

VR technology is embedded in the course, students can acquire knowledge in the way of immersion, interaction, perception and intelligent experience, and learn ideological and political lessons in the way students like, which can effectively solve many problems in college ideological and political lessons. The integration of VR technology into practical teaching has subverted the traditional teaching method based on teaching theory and enriched the teaching content of ideological and political courses. VR technology is not limited by the classroom, makes the content in the textbook more vivid, combines explicit education with implicit education, and extends the classroom through various channels and in various ways, such as: Make full use of the "imagi-nativeness" of VR technology, enhance the learning effect with the way of knowledge transfer, so that students understand that not only learn theoretical knowledge, but more importantly, guide practical activities through theory. In addition, the situation created by teachers in teaching is one of the important methods to test whether students can correctly use relevant knowledge to solve problems. The so-called more real situation, the more help students internalize knowledge.[1] The application of VR technology and practical teaching can stimulate students' internal learning motivation and help them to construct knowledge transfer in virtual scenes.

3.3   Whether Situational Experiential Teaching is Conducive to Improving the Effectiveness of the Educational Process

Theoretical teaching and practical teaching complement each other in ideological and political theory courses in universities. However, due to the restriction of objective con-ditions, many universities ignore practice teaching in teaching, or the effect of practice teaching is not good. Therefore, strengthening the practice teaching of ideological and political theory course is the inevitable requirement of university work. "In the VR vir-tual simulation environment, effectively make up for the shortcomings of traditional classroom teaching, VR virtual simulation to create a personalized learning environ-ment for students, students can ask teachers at any time, teachers and students can freely communicate and interact, enhance the nitiative and participation of students in learn-ing," In the atmosphere of edutainment, it is more conducive for teachers to grasp the problems encountered by students in the first time, so as to better guide students to deal with problems, so as to enhance the effectiveness of students' ideological and political education. The integration of VR technology into the teaching of ideological and polit-ical courses in colleges and universities makes the classroom more colorful, promotes the education and teaching of ideological and political courses closer to reality, closer to life and closer to students, and helps students develop comprehensive literacy. The application of VR technology enables teaching to better expand the space and time of ideological and political education and integrate teaching resources.

The use of VR technology in teaching pays more attention to the subjective needs of students, enhances the interaction between teachers and students, and makes the teaching content more diversified, further enriche students' perception of the world, helps cultivate their thinking ability of seeking knowledge and innovation, and improves the teaching quality. VR virtual reality technology allows students to change from "passive learn-ers" to "active participants", and the teaching content changes from "two-dimensional picture" to "3D three-dimensional experience". VR technology is used to build "vir-tual" and "real" scenes, establish a bridge between teachers and students, and guide college students to enhance emotional experience in the virtual environment. Through the organic integration of VR virtual simulation technology and ideological and polit-ical course teaching, the practice base that is difficult to reach objectively is simulated and constructed with historical events in the past, and the practical teaching content is

---

[1] John Dewey. How we think [M]. Beijing: People's Education Press, 1990:125–126. (in Chinese).

enriched, so as to realize the organic combination of online and offline, virtual and reality, so as to carry out the positive interaction of teaching and present the "sense of reality" of the course.[2] Compared with the traditional ideological and political classroom related carriers, VR virtual simulation also has the characteristics of large information capacity, rich teaching resources, fast transmission speed, wide coverage and so on. "Media integration" into the ideological and political work of colleges and universities, from "face to face" to "key to key". Under the background of "fusion media", the platform of ideological and political education for college students has changed from "one-way communication" to "two-way communication", which has changed the inherent imparting, lack of communication and other defects, and has made an essential leap forward. VR virtual simulation technology is embedded in the practical teaching of ideological and political courses, which makes the ideological and political education of students more three-dimensional, convenient and timely, improves the communication efficiency between teachers and students, and enhances the effectiveness of ideological and political education of college students. In short, the key to the application of VR virtual simulation technology in the teaching of ideological and political courses in colleges and universities lies in the students' true feelings about the scenes created by VR. Only when students are interested in or feel connected with real life can they achieve better educational effects. Therefore, in the face of many difficulties and difficulties in practical teaching of ideological and political courses, through VR virtual simulation teaching platform, a teaching and learning model of "promoting reality with virtual reality and integrating virtual and real" can be constructed to carry out more effective ideological and political education for college students.

4   Conclusion

The integration and development of VR technology and ideological and political theory courses is one of the effective strategies to promote the construction of all-media teaching pattern in universities. VR technology is embedded in the teaching of ideological and political theory courses, which enriches the teaching content of ideological and political courses, expands the teaching form, promotes the process of integrating all media into ideological and political courses, and helps to enhance the effectiveness of ideological and political theory courses teaching.

To sum up, the mode of integrating VR technology into the practical teaching of ideological and political theory courses is an effective way to "tell a good Chinese story". The integration of VR technology into classroom teaching allows students to fully understand the charm contained in the teaching content in the scene experience, perceive the power contained in it, and guide students' confidence in the great rejuvenation of the Chinese nation.

Acknowledgements. This research was supported by The ninth batch of school-level education and teaching reform research and practice projects of Shenzhen Polytechnic of Information Technology (2023djpjgyb28) .

[2] Xie Dongli. Red Culture and the construction of Contemporary College Students' Core Values -- A case study of Zunyi Normal University [J]. Journal of Zunyi Normal University, 2012,14 (03): 5–7.

References

1. John, D.: How we Think, pp. 125–126. People's Education Press, Beijing (1990). (in Chinese)
2. Xie, D.: Red culture and the construction of contemporary college students' core values – a case study of Zunyi normal university. J. Zunyi Normal Univ. **14**(03), 5–7 (2012)
3. Ministry of Education of the People's Republic of China: On the issuance of <The basic work of ideological and political theory teaching in colleges and universities in the new eraRequest> notification. Ministry of Education of the People's Republic of China (2018)
4. Yu, L., Zhou, C.: On the Sinking of China's Higher education Immersion teaching model and practice. Henan Soc. Sci. (06) (2012)

Application of the Metaverse in Product Engineering – A Workshop for Identification of Potential Field of Action

Tobias Düser[(✉)], Maximilian Fischer, Stefan Eric Schwarz, Annika Bastian,
Jonas Freyer, Kristian Vlajic, Matthias Eisenmann, Sven Matthiesen[ID],
and Albert Albers[ID]

IPEK – Institute of Product Engineering, Karlsruhe Institute of Technology (KIT),
Kaiserstr. 10, 76131 Karlsruhe, Germany
tobias.dueser@kit.edu

Abstract. Metaverse will not only change our interpersonal interaction in the future, but also how we develop future products, systems and services. This paper presents five potential fields of action in product engineering regarding the application of the metaverse in product engineering, which were identified in an overarching workshop. For this purpose, different research profiles were determined in the workshop with people of different expertise in product engineering to identify initial research questions and challenges. Research profiles, based on the product profile in product engineering, revealed the following topics of the five potential fields of action: creativity, validation and verification, cross-generational development, Product-Production-CoDesign and education. Human creativity is an important foundation for product development, as it can generate new ideas. This is precisely where potential fields of action exist, for example, in how far the metaverse enables the execution of creativity methods in virtual environment. The metaverse shows potential in validation and verification, as several relevant stakeholders can be integrated with early virtual, physical or hybrid prototypes. Furthermore, products can be represented across generations to ensure circular economy, upgradeability. Here, the metaverse shows potential to access multigenerational products. In addition, the production system can be developed simultaneously with the product itself to correct errors or problems at an early stage. In addition to the direct support of product development, the developers themselves can also be trained in the metaverse by being introduced to new methods, processes and tools by experts. These five potential fields of action need to be further explored in order to better develop or enable services in the metaverse in product development.

Keywords: Metaverse · Product Engineering · Research · Services · Creativity · Generation · Validation and Verification · Production · Education

S. He et al. (Eds.): METAVERSE 2023, LNCS 14210, pp. 39–52, 2023.
https://doi.org/10.1007/978-3-031-44754-9_4

1   Metaverse as an Enabler in Product Engineering

In 2021 Bill Gates stated that "[within] the next two or three years [...] most virtual meetings will move from 2D camera image grids [...] to the metaverse, a 3D space with digital avatars" [1]. The renaming of the Facebook group to Meta Platforms and the launch of the metaverse enabled the usage of the virtual world to make life easier. Nvidia too is aiming for collaboration in a virtual world through the Omniverse [2]. However, it is not only the lives of people or products that will be influenced by the Metaverse in the future, but also the extent to which products, systems and services are developed. Virtual elements are already being used in product development in order to enable prototyping at an early stage or to enable physically distributed development.

Based on several publications, the Fraunhofer Institute defines the metaverse with the following seven characteristics [3]. The metaverse is not a closed system, but networks with each other as well as with reality. It functions as a social medium that allows people to interact, communicate and collaborate with each other while trading and owning property there. The sessions in the Metaverse can be persistent and long-lasting as well as temporary, depending on the individual needs of the users. It is an integrative system that incorporates and leverages other technologies to provide a comprehensive experience. A key action in the Metaverse is to capture user states and the real environment in combination with virtual immersion. Participation in the Metaverse is multimodal and can be adjusted in terms of intensity and representation to suit individual preferences. There is a close linkage with the real world, whereby information, actions and interactions between reality and virtuality can be exchanged and mutually influenced.

These characteristics of the metaverse provide a basis for deriving possible fields of action to be investigated in product engineering. In doing so, needs must be identified where research content must be generated in order to use the metaverse for applications in the development of products, systems and services. In the following chapter, the so-called Research Profile is presented, which describes the needs in research in order to define the potential fields of action.

2   Describing Field of Actions in Research Through Research Profiles

The aim of this publication is to identify potential fields of action that describe possible research fields on how the usage of the metaverse can support the development of products, systems and services. These are described by the Research Profile, which is derived from the Product Profile of product development. The reason for a systematic approach similar to product development is that uncertainties and ambiguities exist in this area and many disciplines are involved. In the following chapter, the basis, the product profile and eating classification, is presented.

2.1   Research Reference: The Product Profile in Innovation Management

Innovations play a crucial role in the success of companies [4]. The term innovation was coined by Schumpeter and refers to the successful introduction of a new technical or organizational change on the market [5]. The evaluation and categorization of an innovation thus can only take place retrospectively, e.g. when the successful introduction to the market has been achieved [6, 7]. Nevertheless, it is of great importance to plan innovations proactively, which is why forward-looking and system-oriented product development serves as the basis for the success of future innovations [8].

Schumpeter's description is taken up by Albers et al. and extended by the product profile [9]. An innovation is described here as the technical implementation of a product profile through an invention and its successful market launch. Innovations can include not only mechatronic products, but also business [10] (Fig. 1).

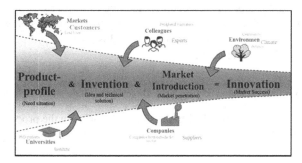

Fig. 1. Understanding innovation according to Albers et al. [9] based on Schumpeter [5]

The product profile is a model of the demand situation that defines the bundle of benefits of a product and provides the scope for product development. It enables the validation of the benefits for providers, customers and users [9]. The development and validation of a product profile is an essential prerequisite for innovation [11]. The product profile is created during the entire development process and validated with the stakeholders involved, both during and after creation [9] (Fig. 2).

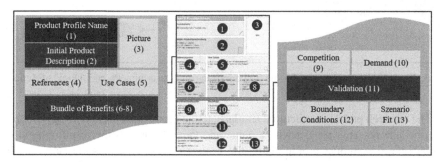

Fig. 2. Scheme of the product profile according to Albers et al. [9]

Therefore, a scheme was developed for modelling product profiles of mechatronic products and for business models [9]. Central aspects of the product profile are the product claim and the bundle of benefits related to the user, customer and supplier.

The claim describes why the product is needed and is formulated with the sentence beginning: "We need a product that…" The benefit bundle describes the intended benefit for the corresponding stakeholder if the product profile is fulfilled. In addition to the two elements, there are product description, references and competitors as well as use cases and demand. The difference between references and competitors is that the former describes possible product solutions and the latter describes concrete products of concrete competitor companies. In addition, validation and constraints are defined by external stakeholders such as law or society.

The product profile describes the need situation and the bundle of benefits of a product, system or service that is being developed. The product profile describes these in a solution-open way. This approach can be adopted in research by defining the need situation and also the bundle of benefits for a specific project. The same, similar or new elements can be described in the research profile. This research profile is described in more detail in the following chapter.

2.2   Research Approach: Identifying and Describing Research Profiles

The research profile can be derived from the product profile. In the process, elements of the product profile are taken over, adapted or new elements are added (Fig. 3).

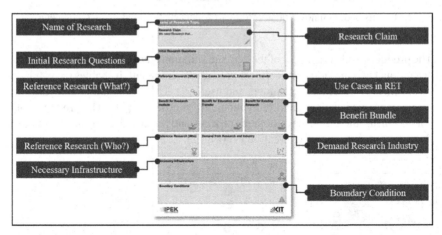

Fig. 3. Template of the Research Profile for Identifying and Describing Potential Field of Actions

The research profile is structured similarly to the product profile. *Name of Research* describes the research project with a name and thus also names the resulting field of action. Like the product profile claim, the *research claim* describes the claim of the research project. It clearly states, what the intended research needs to address and why this research is of importance. The *initial research questions* define first open questions as well as hypotheses that are derived from the claim and have to be substantiated, answered or falsified in further research. *Reference research* refers to existing research projects that are already in progress. Both topics (*What?*) and research institutions such as universities, institutes, etc. (*Who?*) that have defined possible theories, approaches or methods are described. *Use Cases in Research, Education & Transfer* define possible applications in the three fields. In research, specific case studies or research environments can be defined. In transfer, possible cooperations with industrial partners are described in order to then define possible formats in education to introduce students to the topic and to educate them. *Benefit Bundle* describes the resulting benefit for research institutes, education & transfer as well as existing research in the research institutes. *Demand in Research & Industry* provides an assessment of whether and to what extent the current demand for results and findings in this research project is derived from industry or research. *Necessary Infrastructure* describes the necessary infrastructure that a research institute already has but also the one it should have in order to be able to conduct research in the respective field. This makes it possible to quantify the initial effort. *Boundary Condition* shows clear boundaries for the research project. These boundaries can be thematic, domain-specific or similar.

The research profile is only one way to identify and describe potential fields of action. Especially in the context of the metaverse, this is an optimal way to integrate product development experts with the help of a workshop. In this workshop, creativity methods are used to derive, describe and discuss these research profiles. The structure and results of a workshop to identify and describe potential fields of action in the research of support possibilities for the metaverse in engineering are examined in more detail in the following chapter.

3 Workshop Design: Engineering Research for Supporting the Application of Metaverse in Product Engineering

3.1 Preparatory Work: Analyzing Existing Elements of the Metaverse

As it is often the case with trend topics, the metaverse is lacking a universally accepted definition and a clear understanding of who exactly might gain benefits from it [12]. In order to provide an initial overview and therefore to generate a well-balanced knowledge base among the participants, the metaverse has been analysed beforehand. This analysis has been conducted using the structure depicted in Fig. 4.

These eight fields of analysis as well as exemplarily selected findings within these fields are presented below.

- *System in Development* analyses the term metaverse itself and highlights the potentials that arise by interconnecting virtual worlds and (extended) realities with the real world but also amongst themselves [12].
- *User benefits* as well as *Customer benefits* provide insights about the benefits, potential users of the metaverse gain from its usage. Enabling people to teleport as holograms to be present at the office while at the same time cutting down time in traffic and therefore reducing carbon footprints are only some examples [13].
- *Provider benefits* focuses on the benefits, that provides of metaverse platforms such as e. g. Meta or Microsoft [12].
- *Competitors* provides an overview about the extensive competition taking place around the metaverse and its applications. Starting from

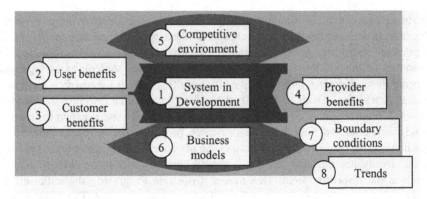

Fig. 4. Search Fields for the Preparation of the Workshop

- *Business models* provides an overview of potential business models that arise with the metaverse. Examples to be mentioned are NFT trading or payment services [14] but also the necessary hardware that enables immersive experiences such as 3D glasses or data gloves [15].
- *Boundary conditions* focuses on the conditions, that need to be fulfilled in order for the metaverse to be successful, where amongst others mainly the needed infrastructure such as high-speed internet but also the necessary hardware to provide immersive experiences are of relevance [16].
- *Trends* highlights elements of the metaverse that are expected to further grow in regards of their respective relevance.

3.2 Workshop Structure: From Research Claims to Research Profiles

After enabling the participants to take part in the workshop by giving them an overview about the topic, the workshop itself was conducted according to the structure depicted in Fig. 5.

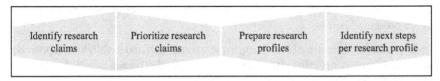

Fig. 5. Overview of the Structured Process of the Conducted Workshop

These four steps are explained in detail below.

- *Identify research claims*
  In order to identify a variety of different research claims, a creativity method called 6–3-5 method has been conducted. Initially intended to be performed by six participants, it has been adapted to fit the varying sizes of the performing teams. By applying this method, a total of nearly 200 potential research claims has been identified.

- *Prioritize research claims*
  As it is impossible to further pursue all 200 research claims, the number of claims is narrowed down. After giving an overview about the two favourite research claims per participant, all participants chose among the various research claims by upvoting their favourite while downvoting their least favourite claims. Using this method, the starting point for the following discussion was set, which finally led to the number of five research claims which are now refined in the third part of the workshop.
- *Prepare research profiles*
  Based on the individual backgrounds of the participants, they have been assigned to a total of five teams, each of which now further refined one of the previously identified research claims. They therefore used the template of the research profile that has been presented in Sect. 2.2. To further enrich the research profiles and to sharpen the field of action that they represent, a variety of different opinions and views has been added by performing the so-called gallery method.
- *Identify next steps per research profile*
  The workshop ended by presenting the finalized research profiles to all participants and defining next steps as well as a responsible for each of the presented fields of action.

4   Workshop Findings: Five Possible Field of Action in Engineering Research for Supporting the Application of Metaverse

In the workshop, a total of five prioritized potential fields of action were identified through research profiles.

4.1   Adapting Creativity Methods in the Early Ideation for Use in the Metaverse

The first field of action identified in the workshop was the use of creativity methods in the metaverse and the following research claim was defined:

We need research that explores methods, processes and tools for creativity-based activities in product development to enable distributed and creative collaboration in the metaverse.

Critical activities in product development – once they take place in a distributed manner – are the activities involving creativity. The joint generation of ideas becomes difficult for teams not working together on-site [17]. Especially for teams that work together fully virtual difficulties in creative processes are a major barrier to successful engineering. Working together in Metaverse could be the solution to this problem [18]. Creativity itself within product engineering is associated with generating something original or new, not necessarily useful. The criterion of being new sets the focus. The distinction between primary and secondary creativity is made to divide the role creativity plays in the product development process. Primary creativity leads to ideas with a high degree of novelty, leading to them having the potential for leading to radical innovations. Secondary creativity has the focus on being useful in the short term without such a high degree of novelty [19]. In product development processes the criterion of being creative in the sense of creating something new that is useful to solve the specific problem is added [20]. Product development can be seen as a problem-solving process consisting of a chain of phases where ideas are generated and then selected. Within this "breathing" process creativity is needed whenever ideas are generated [21]. To support ideation creativity methods can be used, to trigger creativity purposefully by stimulating the human's five senses [22]. Classical creativity methods have been developed for application in person and triggers that might be different (e.g., visual triggers) or non-existing (e.g. habitual triggers) in the virtual application have not been considered. Some creativity methods have already been transferred to virtual use but without the adaptation to the specific needs of a virtual environment [23]. The virtualization of creativity methods has the potential to facilitate and support creative processes since barriers like spatial limitations, lack of resources or time pressure can be overcome [24] (Fig. 6).

Fig. 6. Physical TRIZ-Box with the Items based on the Innovative Principles

Of particular interest here is the use of creativity methods in the Metaverse based on physical elements, such as the TRIZ box. The TRIZ-Box which is a physical support to assist ideation is one of the creativity methods with high potential for being successful within a metaverse application. Consisting of physical objects that represent the 40 innovative principles of TRIZ the TRIZ-Box is currently only suitable for in-person use [22]. Transferring the TRIZ-Box into Metaverse can be used as a first step to study the requirements for transferring in-person creativity methods into successful virtual methods to assist distributed teams and eventually develop a model for the transfer of such methods.

4.2 Building Validation Environment for Early and Continuous Validation and Verification in the Metaverse

The second field of action addresses the validation and verification of products, systems and services in the metaverse, specifically the development of the validation environment in the metaverse:

We need research that explores the description of objectives, requirements and boundary conditions for the validation environment to carry out validation activities in the metaverse.

Validation is the central activity of product development. Validation refers to checking whether a product is suitable for its intended use, achieves the desired value and meets customer requirements. In other words, this is where the question of whether the right product is being developed is answered [25]. This cannot be done by a mere comparison between a partial solution and the specification, since the specification itself must be questioned. For this, the (possibly not yet fully developed) product must be considered in the context of its future use. Verification, on the other hand, is generally understood in the case of technical systems to mean checking whether the actual implementation matches the specification. In other words, it answers the question of whether a product has been developed correctly [25]. The importance of validation in the product development process can be illustrated by "Rule of Ten" for the cost of debugging [26]. This process of integrating validation early in the PDP is also referred to as "frontloading" [27]. In this context, early generation of knowledge can be achieved through early and continuous validation activities. One challenge is that in early phases there is greater uncertainty regarding exact customer requirements as well as use cases [28]. Often, well-defined requirements and use cases for the system or product are not available in early phases, which means that tests cannot be performed or can only be performed with uncertainty. This is exactly where the metaverse offers the possibility to validate product requirements early on by a large number of relevant stakeholders interacting with virtual prototypes. In doing so, existing products can evaluate new product ideas in terms of their fulfillment of the requirement, which also allows the validity of the requirement to be picked up through stakeholder feedback [29]. In addition to stakeholder interaction, further potential exists in the application of the metaverse in validation and verification. For example, by involving the community in validation, the acceptance of the product and system can be increased early on. Additionally, the community can be used to build the validation environment, allowing experts with different backgrounds to create a virtual world. It can also measure how many people have interacted with the product and system, which is important for statistical validation. Finally, the metaverse can be used by the community to find new scenarios of the product or system. Especially the latter is important for the use of autonomous vehicles, where finding new scenarios is an important part [30, 31].

It must be explored how the validation environment, which on the one hand enables interaction with the product and on the other hand represents a realistic environment, is planned, designed and implemented in the different phases. This can enable validation and verification in the metaverse by allowing stakeholders in the metaverse to use the products and identify new application scenarios as they are applied to the product. But new concepts necessary for the product can also be tested, such as teleoperators in the field of autonomous driving. The teleoperators intervene remotely in difficult situations.

4.3 Supporting the Cross-Generational Engineering of Mechatronic Systems in the Metaverse

In the third field of action, intergenerational development and its support is addressed by the metaverse. For this purpose, the following research claim. In the third field of action, intergenerational development and its support is addressed by the metaverse. The following research claim was defined for this purpose:

We need research that explores the modelling of multi-generational products in an environment to enable cross-generational development.

In order to be able to develop products across generations, an approach with the model of PGE – product generation development is introduced. It describes product generation development as the process of developing a new generation of a technical product. Thereby both the adjustment of subsystems and the significant new development of subsystems are considered. The integration of new components into technical products can be realized by variations in form and functional principles. When developing new product generations, reference products are always used to describe the basic structure [32, 33]. In the PGE model, the new product generation is thus based on a reference system whose elements are based on existing products or systems. The development is based on the variation types adoption variation, attribute variation and principle variation [33, 34]. Future development processes and generations can be planned, controlled and managed on the basis of the resulting variation components [35]. These future generations can additionally be planned as well as designed in different horizons by using foresight methods [36].

At this point the metaverse can be a possible support. With the metaverse, the current generations on the market and in development can be represented in order to make the types of variation between the generations and the different variants in the time horizons accessible to the relevant stakeholders.

4.4   Enabling Co-design of Product and Production Systems in the Metaverse

The fourth field of action addresses the integrated Co-design of Products and associated production systems, especially focusing on using the metaverse and its various potentials as enabling technologies. The research claim was therefore summarized as:

We need research that explores the use of the metaverse as an enabler for product-production-codesign (PPCD), to identify errors & potentials in the product development process at an early stage by means of improved simultaneous development.

PPCD comprises iterative planning, development and realization of not only the product but also the associated production system up to the efficient and effective operation of production. It also includes the development of associated business models and the systematic decommissioning of products and production systems while considering several product generations as well as the respective production system evolutions [37]. As it can be seen, lots of the goals pursued by PPCD match with the potentials, the metaverse has to offer. Combining PPCD with the potentials the metaverse has to offer possesses the potential for each field to substantially benefit from one another. Coming back to the identified research claim, the early identification of errors but also of potential does not only rely on having production system data available within the product development and vice versa but it mainly relies on making this data accessible and understandable in an easily comprehensible manner. Using the potentials of the metaverse to visualize the data gathered by e. g. using digital twin technology in an immersive experience may lead to a completely new way of simultaneous product and production system development. Exemplary use cases could e. g. be the following:

- Visualized and immersive impact analysis of changing system parameters
- Early identification of influences the production process has on the product
- Optimization of ergonomics within production processes per individual
- Visualization of motion sequences of workers to optimize the design of future system generations in regards of optimized assembly

While highlighting potential use cases, additional challenges in regards of e. g. usability arise that need to be addressed.

4.5   Teaching Engineering Competences Through Education in the Metaverse

The last field of action relates to the training of tomorrow's developers. Here, the Metaverse can serve as a platform to train the next generation of engineers, to network them and to apply new methods, processes and tools for use in industry, which is why the following research claim was defined:

We need research that explores the use of the metaverse as an enabler for teaching future skills to engineering students to prepare future generations for the use of new methods, processes and tools in product development.

To meet the challenges of the future, such as climate or digitalization, new approaches must be developed, new paths must be taken, or what has existed up to now must be combined in a new way. This requires the formation of new skills and the associated training of young people in these skills, the so-called future skills [38]. These Future Skills describe the skills that will be relevant in the future, as defined in the NextSkills research project [39]. Teaching at universities or other educational institutions must be designed to promote these future skills, making not only technical and expert knowledge relevant in teaching, but also other topics such as well-being, responsibility, mindfulness must be brought closer to students and pupils [38].

This is exactly where Metaverse offers an opportunity to come together virtually, to connect knowledge holders with knowledge seekers, to question and argue, but also to make new teaching concepts accessible to more people, in order to prepare future generations to meet the challenges of the future. One existing opportunity is the CyberLand initiative, where colleges can use the environment to train students and others [40].

5   Summary and Outlook

The metaverse provides an opportunity to improve development of products, systems and services in the future. As the fields of action show, several people can be brought together in the metaverse to create new ideas in virtual space using creative methods, for example, or to validate new inventions and their requirements in virtual validation environments. In addition, the metaverse gives us the opportunity to design multigenerational products and systems as well as their services in one environment in order to define development leaps. Not only the product, system and service itself can be developed, but also the production system, which can be developed simultaneously and consistently through the metaverse and its elements. Last but not least, the metaverse gives a possibility to educate the future generations in product development in order to teach the Future Skills. New teaching formats and contents can be integrated in the metaverse and a larger number of students and pupils can be reached.

The potential fields of action presented need to be further concretized and challenges derived. For example, the virtualization of the TRIZ-Box can generate knowledge about the challenges, potentials and stumbling blocks in the virtualization of creativity methods. In addition, use cases must be defined that are interesting for validation in the metaverse, which may also make cross-generational product development relevant. Furthermore, the goals of the Product-Production-CoDesign should be determined in order to compare them with the goals of the Metaverse. In this way, commonalities and potentials can be identified, while at the same time new challenges arise. These challenges need to be addressed in order to further concretize the fields of action.

References

1. Gates, B.: Reasons for optimism after a difficult year. 2021 gave us a preview of our more digitized future. https://www.gatesnotes.com/Year-in-Review-2021#ALChapter5 (2021). Accessed 2 Jul 2023
2. NVIDIA: NVIDIA Omniverse. https://www.nvidia.com/en-us/omniverse/ (2023). Accessed 2 Jul 2023
3. Laß, D.: Technologien und Use Cases für das (Industrial) Metaverse. Fakt oder Fiktion? (Engl. Technologies and Use Cases for the (Industrial) Metaverse. Fact or Fiction?). Fraunhofer-Verbund IUK-Technologie (2022)
4. Schuh, G.: Innovationsmanagement. Handbuch Produktion und Management 3, 2nd edn. VDI-Buch. Springer Berlin Heidelberg, Berlin, Heidelberg (2012)
5. Schumpeter, J.A.: Business Cycles. A Theoretical, Historical, and Statistical Analysis of the Capitalist Process. McGraw-Hill, New York (1939)
6. Albers, A., Bursac, N., Wintergerst, E.: Product generation development – importance and challenges from a design research perspective. In: New Developments in Mechanics and Mechanical Engineering, pp. 16–21 (2015)
7. Albers, A., et al.: Produktgeneration 1 im Modell der PGE – Produktgenerationsentwicklung: Verständnis, Zusammenhänge und Auswirkungen in der Produktentwicklung. Verständnis, Zusammenhänge und Auswirkungen in der Produktentwicklung. KIT Scientific Working Papers, 149, Karlsruhe (2020)
8. Albers, A., Gausemeier, J.: Von der fachdisziplinorientierten Produktentwicklung zur Vorausschauenden und Systemorientierten Produktentstehung. In: Anderl, R., Eigner, M., Sendler, U., Stark, R. (eds.) Smart Engineering. acatech DISKUSSION, pp. 17–29. Springer Berlin Heidelberg, Berlin (2012)
9. Albers, A., et al.: Product profiles: modelling customer benefits as a foundation to bring inventions to innovations. In: Laroche, F., Bernard, A. (eds.) Proceedings of the 28th CIRP Design Conference (CIRP), pp. 253–258. Konferenz, Nantes, Frankreich (2018)
10. Albers, A., Basedow, G., Heimicke, J., Marthaler, F., Spadinger, M., Rapp, S.: Developing a common understanding of business models from the product development perspective. In: Procedia 30th CIRP Design Conference, pp. 875–882 (2020)

11. Albers, A., et al.: Managing systems of objectives in the agile development of mechatronic systems by ASD – agile systems design. In: The Design Society (ed.) Proceedings of Nord-Design 2018. Design in the Era of Digitalization. NordDesign 2018, 14–17 Aug. The Design Society, Linköping, Schweden (2018)
12. Fraunhofer-Verbund IUK-Technologie: Technologien und Use Cases für das (Industrial) Metaverse. https://www.iuk.fraunhofer.de/content/dam/iuk/de/Download/Technolog ien%20und%20Use%20Cases%20f%C3%BCr%20das%20(Industrial)%20Metaverse.pdf. Accessed 6 Jul 2023
13. Meta: Founder's Letter. https://about.fb.com/news/2021/10/founders-letter/ (2023). Accessed 6 Jul 2023
14. Binance: Why NFTs Are The Keys To Accessing The Metaverse. https://www.binance. com/en/blog/nft/why-nfts-are-the-keys-to-accessing-the-metaverse-421499824684903085 (2021). Accessed 6 Jul 2023
15. Rospigliosi, P.: Metaverse or Simulacra? Roblox, Minecraft, Meta and the turn to virtual reality for education, socialisation and work. In: Interactive Learning Environments (2022). https://doi.org/10.1080/10494820.2022.2022899
16. Tayal, S., Rajagopal, K., Mahajan, V.: Virtual reality based metaverse of gamification. In: 2022 6th International Conference on Computing Methodologies and Communication (ICCMC). 2022 6th International Conference on Computing Methodologies and Communication (ICCMC), Erode, India, 29 Mar 2022 – 31 Mar 2022, pp. 1597–1604. IEEE (2022). https://doi.org/10.1109/ICCMC53470.2022.9753727
17. Brucks, M.S., Levav, J.: Virtual communication curbs creative idea generation. Nature (2022). https://doi.org/10.1038/s41586-022-04643-y
18. Alahuhta, P., Nordbäck, E., Sivunen, A., Surakka, T.: Fostering team creativity in virtual worlds. JVWR (2014). https://doi.org/10.4101/jvwr.v7i3.7062
19. Kreativität des Konstrukteurs (1985)
20. Gramann, J.: Problemmodelle und Bionik als Methode, Technische Universität München. https://mediatum.ub.tum.de/601901 (2004)
21. Albers, A., Braun, A.: Der Prozess der Produktentstehung. In: Henning, F., Moeller, E. (eds.) Handbuch Leichtbau. Methoden, Werkstoffe, Fertigung. Hanser eLibrary, 2nd edn. Hanser, München (2011)
22. Albers, A., Deigendesch, T., Schmalenbach, H.: TRIZ-box–Improving creativity by connecting TRIZ and artifacts. Proc. Eng. (2011). https://doi.org/10.1016/j.proeng.2011.03.113
23. Gräßler, I., Taplick, P.: Virtual Reality unterstützte Kreativitätstechnik: Vergleich mit klassischen Techniken. In: Krause, D., Paetzold, K., Wartzack, S. (eds.) Design for X – Beiträge zum 29. DfX-Symposium, pp. 215–226 (2018)
24. Head Mounted Displays in deutschen Unternehmen. Ein Virtual, Augmented und Mixed Reality Check (2016)
25. Verein Deutscher Ingenieure e. V.: VDI-Richtlinie 2221 Blatt 1 Entwicklung technischer Produkte und Systeme Modell der Produktentwicklung (2019). Accessed 19 Jan 2023
26. Ehrlenspiel, K., Meerkamm, H.: Integrierte Produktentwicklung: Denkabläufe, Methodeneinsatz, Zusammenarbeit. 3 (2009)
27. Raghupatruni, I., Goeppel, T., Atak, M., Bou, J., Huber, T.: Empirical testing of automotive cyber-physical systems with credible software-in-the-loop environments. In: 2019 IEEE International Conference on Connected Vehicles and Expo (ICCVE). IEEE (2019). https://doi.org/10.1109/iccve45908.2019.8965169
28. Muschik, S.: Development of systems of objectives in early product engineering. Entwicklung von Zielsystemen in der frühen Produktentstehung. In: Albers, A. (ed.) Forschungsberichte des IPEK – Institut für Produktentwicklung. Systeme, Methoden, Prozesse, Karlsruhe (2011)
29. Richter, T., et al.: Pitch 2.0–Concept of early evaluation of product profiles in product generation engineering. In: Horvath, I., Suarez, J.P. (eds.) Proceedings of TMCE 2018 (2018)

30. Düser, T.: Verfahren zum Testen eines Fahrerassistenzsystems eines Fahrzeugs Patent AT524822A1
31. Düser, T.: Verfahren und System zum Erzeugen von Szenariendaten zum Testen eines Fahrerassistenzsystems eines Fahrzeugs Patent AT524821A1
32. Albers, A., et al.: The reference system in the model of PGE: proposing a generalized description of reference products and their interrelations. In: Wartzack, S., Schleich, B. (eds.) Proceedings of the 22nd international conference on engineering design (ICED19). 22nd International Conference on Engineering Design (ICED19), Delft, Netherland, 5–8 Aug 2019, pp. 1693–1702 (2019). https://doi.org/10.5445/IR/1000097325
33. Albers, A., Bursac, N., Wintergerst E.: Product generation development – importance and challenges from a design research perspective. New Dev. Mech. Mech. Eng. 16–21 (2015)
34. Albers, A., et al.: Product generation development - importance and challenges from a design research perspective. Proc. Des. Soc.: Des. Conf. (2020). https://doi.org/10.1017/dsd.2020.315
35. Albers, A., Bursac, N., Urbanec, J., Lüdecke, R., Rachenkova, G.: Knowledge management in product generation development – an empirical study. In: Krause, D., Paetzold, K., Wartzack, S. (eds.) Design for X. Beiträge zum 25. DfX-Symposium, Oktober 2014, pp. 13–24. TuTech Verlag TuTech Innovation GmbH, Hamburg (2014)
36. Albers, A., Marthaler, F., Schlegel, M., Thümmel, C., Kübler, M., Siebe, A.: Eine Systematik zur zukunftsorientierten Produktentwicklung: Generationsübergreifende Ableitung von Produktprofilen zukünftiger Produktgenerationen durch strategische Vorausschau (2022)
37. Albers, A., et al.: Product-production-codesign: an approach on integrated product and production engineering across generations and life cycles. Proc. CIRP (2022). https://doi.org/10.1016/j.procir.2022.05.231
38. Ehlers, U.-D.: Future Skills. Lernen der Zukunft - Hochschule der Zukunft. Zukunft der Hochschulbildung - Future Higher Education. Springer VS, Wiesbaden, Heidelberg (2020)
39. Next Skills: Home – Next Skills. https://nextskills.org/ (2023). Accessed 5 July 2023
40. Fraunhofer-Institut für Arbeitswirtschaft und Organisation IAO: CyberLänd: Baden-Württemberg auf dem Weg ins Metaverse. https://www.iao.fraunhofer.de/de/presse-und-medien/aktuelles/cyberlaend-baden-wuerttemberg-auf-dem-weg-ins-metaverse.html (2023). Accessed 12 July 2023

Application and Industry Track

Carbon Neutrality in Smart Tech-Parks: Leveraging Metaverse and Energy Management Application

Xuejiao Pang[1]([✉]), Xiaohu Fan[1,2,3] [iD], Xing Lu[1], Yi Li[4], and Jie Han[1]

[1] Wuhan Collage, Wuhan, Hubei 430070, P. R. China
9452@whxy.edu.cn
[2] Wuhan Tuspark Hezhong Science and Technology Develop Co. Ltd., Wuhan 430074, China
[3] Wuhan Bohu Science and Technology Co. Ltd., Wuhan 430070, China
[4] Shenzhen Institute of Information Technology, Shenzhen 518000, China

Abstract. This study aims to achieve carbon neutrality in smart tech-parks by leveraging the synergistic integration of digital twin and energy management technologies. By creating a virtual replica of the physical park through digital twin technology, coupled with advanced energy management techniques, this research strives to optimize energy utilization, minimize carbon emissions, and enhance sustainability. Innovative approaches are proposed for improving energy efficiency, demand response, and integrating renewable energy sources within the park infrastructure. Real-time data from IoT devices and sensors are seamlessly integrated into the digital twin, enabling continuous monitoring, analysis, and control of energy systems. This dynamic energy management approach facilitates the achievement of carbon neutrality by ensuring a balance between energy generation and consumption. Experimental evaluations and simulations are conducted to assess the effectiveness and feasibility of the proposed methods, with results showcasing a significant reduction in energy consumption and carbon emissions, achieving an impressive 86% accuracy rate in carbon neutrality. The findings contribute to the field of sustainable smart tech-parks, providing valuable insights into the integration of digital twin and energy management technologies for achieving carbon neutrality. This research offers practical guidance for park operators, policymakers, and researchers involved in the development and management of smart tech-parks.

Keywords: Carbon Neutrality · Smart Tech-parks · Metaverse · Renewable Energy Integration · IoT · Dynamic Energy Balancing

1 Introduction

1.1 Background

Smart tech-parks have emerged as key components of urban development, integrating technology, innovation, and industry. However, the increasing energy demands and environmental concerns associated with these parks pose significant challenges [1]. Achieving carbon neutrality and efficient energy management are crucial for the sustainable development of smart tech-parks.

© The Author(s), under exclusive license to Springer Nature Switzerland AG 2023
S. He et al. (Eds.): METAVERSE 2023, LNCS 14210, pp. 55–70, 2023.
https://doi.org/10.1007/978-3-031-44754-9_5

1.2 Research Problem and Objectives

The challenges in energy management and carbon neutrality in smart tech-parks include dynamic energy demands, uneven energy distribution, and the limitations of traditional energy systems [2]. This research aims to address these challenges by leveraging digital twin and energy management technologies. The primary objectives are to optimize energy utilization, achieve dynamic energy balance, and promote carbon neutrality within smart tech-parks.

1.3 Significance of the Study

This study contributes to the field of smart tech-parks by proposing innovative solutions for energy management and carbon neutrality. The integration of digital twin technology allows for real-time monitoring and control, enabling efficient energy distribution and utilization. The findings and methodologies from this research provide practical insights for policymakers, park operators, and researchers involved in the development and management of smart tech-parks.

2 Related Works

2.1 Digital Twin Technology

Digital twin technology is a key enabler for the development of smart tech-parks. This section reviews the fundamental principles and concepts of digital twin technology, including its definition, components, and applications [3]. The literature review highlights the role of digital twin in enhancing energy management and carbon neutrality within smart tech-parks [4].

2.2 Energy Management in Smart Tech-Parks

Effective energy management is essential for optimizing energy utilization and reducing carbon emissions in smart tech-parks. This section reviews the existing literature on energy management techniques, including demand-side management, energy monitoring and control, renewable energy integration, and energy efficiency improvement strategies. The review emphasizes the importance of intelligent energy management systems in achieving carbon neutrality.

2.3 Research Progress in the Field

In the field of energy management and carbon neutrality in smart tech-parks, researchers and institutions worldwide have conducted extensive and in-depth studies. The following provides an academic overview of the research progress in this area:

2.3.1 Energy Management Research

In energy management, numerous studies have focused on developing intelligent monitoring, control, and optimization methods [5]. Researchers worldwide have employed technologies such as sensor networks, IoT, and data analytics to achieve real-time energy consumption monitoring and analysis [6]. Additionally, they have explored energy consumption prediction models and optimization algorithms to improve energy utilization efficiency and reduce waste [7].

2.3.2 Carbon Neutrality Assessment Research

In the area of carbon neutrality assessment, scholars have been devoted to developing scientifically accurate assessment methods and indicators to measure the effectiveness of carbon emissions reduction and the sustainability of energy management in tech-parks [8]. They have utilized tools such as system dynamics models, life cycle assessment methods, and carbon footprint analysis to quantitatively analyze carbon emission sources, carbon reduction potentials, and carbon neutrality targets, providing decision-makers with scientific guidance [9].

2.3.3 Energy Demand Forecasting and Allocation Optimization Research

To achieve dynamic energy balance and carbon neutrality goals in smart tech-parks, researchers have proposed various energy demand forecasting and allocation optimization methods. Statistical and machine learning-based energy demand prediction models have made significant advancements in terms of accuracy and real-time capabilities [10]. Moreover, optimization algorithms such as genetic algorithms and particle swarm optimization have been applied to energy allocation problems, maximizing energy efficiency and carbon emissions reduction while meeting energy demand [11].

2.3.4 Security and Privacy Protection Research

The digital twin systems in smart tech-parks involve sensitive data and critical information, making security and privacy protection paramount. Scholars have proposed various security and privacy protection mechanisms [12], such as data encryption, access control, and anonymization methods, to ensure data security and user privacy in the digital twin systems [13].

In summary, significant progress has been made in energy management and carbon neutrality research in smart tech-parks both domestically and internationally. However, challenges remain, including data quality and reliability, algorithm accuracy, and real-time capabilities. Therefore, this study aims to further explore and improve algorithms and methods in energy management and carbon neutrality based on existing research, contributing to the sustainable development of smart tech-parks.

2.4   Research Gaps and Contributions

Based on the literature review, this section identifies the research gaps and limitations in the existing studies. It highlights the need for further research in areas such as the integration of digital twin technology with energy management systems, dynamic energy balancing algorithms, and real-time monitoring for carbon neutrality. The section also outlines the contributions of this research in addressing these research gaps.

3   Smart Tech-Parks and Energy Management

Before any work can begin, it is necessary to construct a digital foundation by leveraging GIS technology, unmanned aerial vehicles (UAVs) for oblique photography, 3D modeling, and other techniques. The existing park area is digitally reconstructed and restored to a certain scale and accuracy through digital modeling. Subsequently, various equipment and scenarios are associated with the digital model. The hierarchical architecture of the system is shown in Fig. 1.

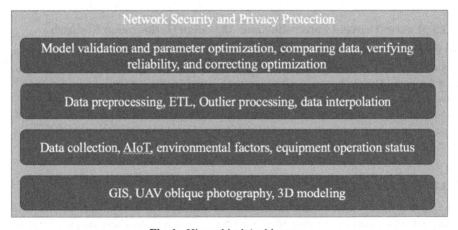

Fig. 1. Hierarchical Architecture.

3.1   Smart Tech-Parks: Concepts and Characteristics

3.1.1   Definition and Evolution of Smart Tech-Parks

This section provides a detailed overview of the concept and definition of smart tech-parks, including their origins, evolutionary process, and notable case studies both domestically and internationally. It emphasizes the goals and mission of smart tech-parks and their role in promoting economic growth, innovation, and sustainable development.

3.1.2 Characteristics and Elements of Smart Tech-Parks

Smart tech-parks possess distinct characteristics and elements. This section explores their key characteristics, including digitization and intelligence, industrial integration and innovation ecosystems, and sustainability. It also analyzes the critical elements of smart tech-parks, such as infrastructure development, the establishment of innovation ecosystems, and talent cultivation, and their impact on energy management.

3.2 Importance of Energy Management in Smart Tech-Parks

3.2.1 Concepts and Objectives of Energy Management

This section introduces the fundamental concepts and objectives of energy management, including improving energy efficiency, reducing carbon emissions, and optimizing energy supply and demand balance. It emphasizes the significance of energy management in smart tech-parks to achieve sustainable development and carbon neutrality goals.

3.2.2 Challenges in Energy Management for Smart Tech-Parks

Smart tech-parks face various challenges in energy management. This section thoroughly analyzes these challenges, such as fluctuating energy demands, unstable energy supply, and low energy efficiency. Furthermore, it discusses the implications of these challenges on sustainable development and the achievement of carbon neutrality goals in smart tech-parks.

3.3 Application of Digital Twin Technology

3.3.1 Fundamentals of Digital Twin Technology

This section introduces the basic principles of digital twin technology, encompassing the construction of digital twin models, data acquisition and processing, and model validation and updating. It highlights the potential applications of digital twin technology in energy management, including real-time monitoring, predictive analysis, and optimization control.

3.3.2 Specific Applications of Digital Twin Technology in Energy Management of Smart Tech-Parks

This section delves into the specific applications of digital twin technology in energy management of smart tech-parks. It covers aspects such as energy system modeling and simulation, intelligent energy monitoring and control, and energy optimization and dynamic balance. Emphasis is placed on the innovative applications of digital twin technology in achieving energy efficiency improvement and carbon neutrality goals.

3.4 Key Technologies and Methods in Energy Management

There are six main factors related to the core concept of dual carbon system management, as shown in Fig. 2. We will elaborate on the specific details in this chapter.

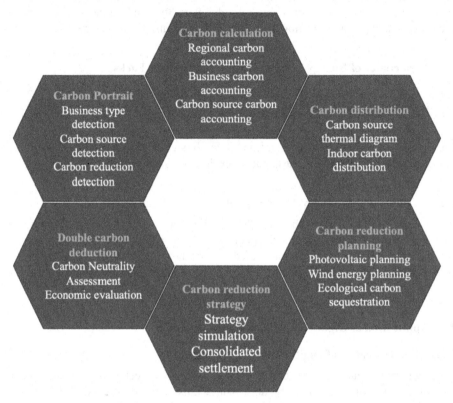

Fig. 2. Global dual carbon management system.

3.4.1 Energy Data Acquisition and Monitoring Technologies

This section discusses the latest developments and applications of energy data acquisition and monitoring technologies, including sensor networks, smart metering systems, and remote monitoring and control. It analyzes the utilization of these technologies in energy management of smart tech-parks and their impact on energy decision-making and optimization.

3.4.2 Energy Demand Prediction Algorithms

To address the fluctuating energy demands in smart tech-parks, this section presents the principles and methods of energy demand prediction algorithms. It includes statistical models, machine learning, and deep learning-based prediction algorithms and examines their applicability and accuracy in energy management of smart tech-parks.

3.4.3 Energy Allocation Optimization Methods

To achieve energy supply and demand balance and improve energy efficiency, this section explores the research progress in energy allocation optimization methods. It covers dynamic programming, optimization algorithms, and artificial intelligence techniques for energy allocation strategies. The section emphasizes the application of these methods in energy management of smart tech-parks and their contributions to energy optimization and carbon neutrality goals.

3.5 Case Studies and Lessons Learned

This section presents practical case studies in energy management of smart tech-parks and summarizes the lessons learned and successful experiences. It analyzes the technologies, methods, and strategies employed in these case studies and examines the challenges and solutions encountered during the implementation process. Best practice guidelines for energy management in smart tech-parks are derived from the lessons learned in these case studies.

4 Metaverse-Enabled Energy Management

This chapter introduces the application of digital twin technology in energy management for achieving carbon neutrality in smart tech-parks. It outlines the objectives of the chapter and provides an overview of the topics covered. The principles and architecture of the system are shown in Fig. 3.

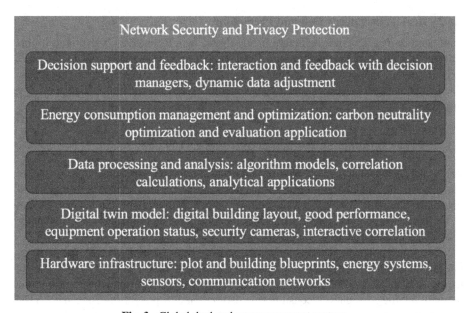

Fig. 3. Global dual carbon management system.

4.1 Digital Twin Modeling for Energy Systems

4.1.1 Digital Twin Model Construction

This section details the process of constructing digital twin models for energy systems in smart tech-parks. It discusses the selection of system components, data acquisition and integration, and model validation techniques. Emphasis is placed on the incorporation of real-time data from IoT devices through the integration with the AIoT platform.

4.1.2 Virtual Representation and Simulation

Here, the virtual representation and simulation capabilities of digital twin models are explored. It discusses the utilization of physics-based and data-driven modeling techniques to accurately simulate the behavior of energy systems in real-time. The importance of model accuracy and fidelity for effective energy management is highlighted.

4.2 Energy Demand Prediction Using Digital Twins

4.2.1 Energy Demand Forecasting Models

This section presents various energy demand forecasting models that can be applied within the context of digital twin-enabled energy management. It discusses statistical models, machine learning algorithms, and hybrid approaches. The selection criteria for choosing the appropriate model based on data availability and prediction accuracy are discussed.

4.2.2 Real-Time Energy Demand Prediction

Real-time energy demand prediction using digital twin technology is explored in this section. It highlights the integration of real-time data from sensors and IoT devices into the digital twin model to enable accurate and timely energy demand forecasts. The challenges and considerations in implementing real-time prediction algorithms are discussed.

4.3 Energy Consumption Prediction Based on LSTM

Based on historical energy consumption data and relevant influencing factors, we utilize energy consumption prediction algorithms to forecast the future energy consumption of the smart tech-park. By establishing a model that incorporates specific factors relevant to the park, we can accurately predict the energy consumption trends and demands, providing valuable reference for energy optimization.

The proposed method utilizes the Long Short-Term Memory (LSTM) algorithm, which is a popular recurrent neural network model known for its ability to effectively handle sequential data and capture temporal dependencies. The following steps outline the methodology for energy consumption estimation and prediction using the LSTM algorithm:

Data Preparation: Collect and organize historical energy consumption data and the corresponding influencing factors, such as temperature, humidity, and working hours. Divide the data into training and testing sets.

Feature Engineering: Preprocess and extract features from the data. Techniques such as standardization, normalization, and feature engineering methods like sliding windows and differencing can be applied to enhance the data representation.

LSTM Model Construction: Construct an LSTM model for energy consumption estimation and prediction. The LSTM model consists of input, hidden, and output layers. Fine-tune the hyperparameters, including the number of neurons, layers, learning rate, as well as selecting an appropriate loss function and optimizer to improve the model's accuracy and generalization capability.

Model Training: Train the LSTM model using the training dataset. During the training process, feed the historical energy consumption data and relevant influencing factors into the LSTM model and update the model parameters through backpropagation based on the actual energy consumption. Repeat this process for multiple training epochs until the model converges.

Model Prediction: Utilize the trained LSTM model to predict and estimate energy consumption using the testing dataset. Input the testing data into the LSTM model and use forward propagation to obtain the predicted energy consumption results.

Model Evaluation: Evaluate the predicted results by calculating the errors between the predicted energy consumption and the actual energy consumption. Common evaluation metrics such as Root Mean Square Error (RMSE), Mean Absolute Error (MAE), and correlation coefficients can be used to assess the performance of the model.

Model Optimization: Based on the evaluation results, optimize the LSTM model by adjusting its structure, hyperparameters, and training strategies to improve its performance and prediction accuracy.

The proposed energy consumption estimation and prediction method based on the LSTM algorithm can effectively handle time series data and provide accurate energy consumption forecasts. By properly preparing the data, performing feature engineering, and training the LSTM model, it can offer valuable support for energy management and optimization in smart tech-parks.

4.4   Energy Allocation Optimization with Metaverse

4.4.1   Optimization Framework and Objective Functions

This section presents an optimization framework for energy allocation in smart tech-parks using digital twins. It discusses the formulation of objective functions that consider energy efficiency, cost minimization, and carbon emissions reduction. Different optimization techniques, such as linear programming and metaheuristic algorithms, are explored.

The Carbon Neutrality Assessment Algorithm aims to evaluate the carbon neutrality progress in a smart tech-park and calculate the carbon neutrality index to measure the effectiveness of carbon emission reduction efforts and the sustainability of energy management. This algorithm considers factors such as energy consumption, carbon emissions, and energy efficiency to provide a comprehensive assessment of the carbon neutrality level (see Table 1).

Table 1. Algorithm Steps

Steps	Discription
1	Collect energy consumption data and carbon emissions data, as well as other relevant metrics associated with energy management
2	Calculate the energy efficiency, which is the ratio of energy output to energy consumption
3	Compute the carbon intensity, which represents the amount of carbon emissions per unit of energy consumption
4	Calculate the carbon neutrality index for the smart tech-park by combining the weighted contributions of energy efficiency and carbon intensity. The weights can be determined based on specific criteria or standards
5	Assess the carbon neutrality level of the tech-park based on the computed carbon neutrality index. A threshold or criteria can be set to determine whether the carbon neutrality goal has been achieved
6	Present the assessment results and relevant metrics in a visual format for comparison and analysis

4.4.2 Constraints and Optimization Algorithms

Here, the constraints involved in energy allocation optimization are discussed, including physical constraints, operational constraints, and environmental constraints. Various optimization algorithms, such as genetic algorithms, particle swarm optimization, and mixed-integer linear programming, are presented and compared in terms of their applicability and performance.

4.5 Case Studies and Results

This section presents case studies that demonstrate the application of digital twin-enabled energy management for carbon neutrality in smart tech-parks. It discusses the specific scenarios, data collection methods, model implementation, and optimization results. The performance evaluation metrics and analysis of the achieved energy efficiency and carbon reduction are presented.

4.6 Discussion and Insights

The discussion section analyzes the results obtained from the case studies and provides insights into the effectiveness and limitations of digital twin-enabled energy management. It discusses the key factors influencing the performance of the system and identifies areas for further improvement. The potential for scalability and transferability of the proposed approach to other smart tech-parks is also discussed.

5 Security and Privacy Protection i

In this chapter, we focus on the crucial aspect of security and privacy protection in digital twin-enabled energy management for smart tech-parks. We discuss the potential security threats and privacy challenges faced in the implementation of digital twin technology and propose effective strategies to mitigate these risks.

5.1 Security Threats in Digital Twin-Enabled Energy Management

5.1.1 Threats to Data Integrity and Availability

This section explores the potential threats to data integrity and availability in the context of digital twin-enabled energy management. It discusses attacks such as data tampering, unauthorized data access, and denial-of-service (DoS) attacks. The impact of these threats on energy management and potential consequences are analyzed.

5.1.2 Cybersecurity Risks in Energy Systems

Here, we examine the cybersecurity risks that arise in the energy systems of smart tech-parks. This includes vulnerabilities in control systems, communication networks, and IoT devices. We discuss the potential consequences of cyber-attacks on energy infrastructure and the importance of robust security measures.

5.2 Privacy Challenges in Digital Twin Technology

5.2.1 Data Privacy and Confidentiality

This section addresses the privacy challenges associated with digital twin technology. It discusses the collection, storage, and utilization of sensitive data in the digital twin ecosystem. The importance of protecting individual privacy, complying with data protection regulations, and ensuring data confidentiality are emphasized.

5.2.2 Privacy-Preserving Techniques

We delve into privacy-preserving techniques that can be applied in digital twin-enabled energy management. This includes methods such as data anonymization, encryption, and secure multi-party computation. The advantages and limitations of these techniques in preserving privacy while maintaining data utility are discussed.

5.3 Security and Privacy Measures

5.3.1 Authentication and Access Control

This section focuses on authentication and access control mechanisms to ensure secure access to digital twin systems. It discusses techniques such as strong user authentication, role-based access control, and two-factor authentication. The role of access control in protecting against unauthorized access and data breaches is highlighted.

5.3.2   Data Encryption and Secure Communication

Here, we explore the use of data encryption and secure communication protocols to protect data confidentiality and integrity in digital twin-enabled energy management. We discuss encryption algorithms, secure communication protocols (such as SSL/TLS), and key management strategies to safeguard data transmission.

5.3.3   Monitoring and Intrusion Detection

This section addresses the importance of monitoring and intrusion detection systems in detecting and mitigating security threats. It discusses techniques such as network monitoring, anomaly detection, and intrusion detection systems (IDS) to identify potential attacks and respond proactively.

5.4   Case Studies and Best Practices

This section presents case studies and best practices that demonstrate effective security and privacy measures in digital twin-enabled energy management. It discusses real-world implementations, challenges faced, and the lessons learned from these cases. The emphasis is on identifying successful strategies and approaches to ensure robust security and privacy protection, as shown in Fig. 4.

Fig. 4. Case study of Metaverse based global dual carbon management system.

5.5   Future Trends and Research Directions

The chapter concludes with an outlook on future trends and research directions in security and privacy protection for digital twin-enabled energy management. It highlights the need for ongoing advancements in security technologies, privacy-enhancing mechanisms, and the integration of AI and machine learning for proactive threat detection.

6   Experimental Setup and Results

In this chapter, we present the experimental setup, data collection, and analysis of results for the digital twin-enabled energy management system in a smart tech-park. We discuss the objectives of the experiments and provide an overview of the methodologies employed.

6.1   Experimental Setup

6.1.1   Testbed Description

This section provides a detailed description of the testbed used for conducting the experiments. It includes information about the smart tech-park infrastructure, energy systems, and the deployed digital twin model. The hardware and software components used in the experimental setup are also discussed.

6.1.2   Data Collection and Monitoring

Here, we explain the process of data collection and monitoring in the smart tech-park. It covers the selection of sensors, data acquisition methods, and the integration of data into the digital twin model. The frequency and duration of data collection, as well as the specific energy parameters monitored, are highlighted.

6.2   Experimental Methodology

6.2.1   Energy Demand Prediction Experiment

This section describes the experimental methodology for energy demand prediction using the digital twin-enabled energy management system. It outlines the data preprocessing steps, model training and validation techniques, and the evaluation metrics used to assess the accuracy of the predictions.

6.2.2   Energy Allocation Optimization Experiment

Here, we outline the experimental methodology for energy allocation optimization in the smart tech-park. It discusses the formulation of the optimization problem, the selection of objective functions and constraints, and the optimization algorithms employed. The evaluation metrics used to measure the effectiveness of the optimization process are presented.

6.3   Results and Analysis

6.3.1   Energy Demand Prediction Results

This section presents the results of the energy demand prediction experiments. It provides an analysis of the prediction accuracy, comparing the predicted energy demand values with the actual values. The factors influencing the prediction performance and the implications for energy management are discussed.

6.3.2 Energy Allocation Optimization Results

Here, we present the results of the energy allocation optimization experiments. It includes an analysis of the optimized energy allocation plans, comparing them with the baseline scenarios. The achieved energy efficiency improvements, cost reductions, and carbon emissions reductions are quantified and discussed.

6.4 Discussion and Interpretation

The discussion section provides a comprehensive interpretation of the experimental results. It analyzes the implications of the findings, highlights the strengths and limitations of the digital twin-enabled energy management system, and identifies areas for further improvement. The insights gained from the experiments are discussed in the context of achieving carbon neutrality in the smart tech-park.

6.5 Case Study and Real-World Implementation

This section presents a case study and real-world implementation of the digital twin-enabled energy management system in a specific smart tech-park. It discusses the practical challenges faced during the implementation, the integration with existing infrastructure, and the lessons learned. The case study provides valuable insights into the feasibility and effectiveness of the proposed system. In real applications, all equipment data in the park are closely linked with the Metaverse system, and the update interval is less than one minute, as shown in Fig. 5. The actual operation of the monitoring center is shown in Fig. 6, which is displayed in conjunction with other monitoring equipment in the duty center.

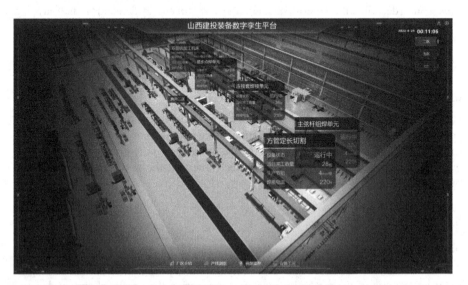

Fig. 5. IoT equipment data interactive with the Metaverse system.

Fig. 6. Real deployment and operation scenarios

6.6 Conclusion

The conclusion summarizes the key findings and contributions of the experimental study. It emphasizes the significance of the results in advancing the field of digital twin-enabled energy management and highlights future research directions. The chapter concludes with a reflection on the overall achievements and the potential impact of the research on achieving carbon neutrality in smart tech-parks.

References

1. Zhu, H., Goh, H.H., Zhang, D., et al.: Key technologies for smart energy systems: recent developments, challenges, and research opportunities in the context of carbon neutrality. J. Clean. Prod. **331**, 129809 (2022)
2. Liao, H., Zhou, Z., Liu, N., et al.: Cloud-edge-device collaborative reliable and communication-efficient digital twin for low-carbon electrical equipment management. IEEE Trans. Industr. Inf. **19**(2), 1715–1724 (2022)
3. Dulaimi, A., Hamida, R., Naser, M., et al.: Digital twin solution implemented on energy hub to foster sustainable smart energy city, case study of sustainable smart energy hub. ISPRS Ann. Photogrammetry, Remote Sens. Spat. Inf. Sci. **10**, 41–48 (2022)
4. Bhatti, G., Mohan, H., Singh, R.R.: Towards the future of smart electric vehicles: digital twin technology. Renew. Sustain. Energy Rev. **141**, 110801 (2021)
5. Kim, H., Choi, H., Kang, H., et al.: A systematic review of the smart energy conservation system: from smart homes to sustainable smart cities. Renew. Sustain. Energy Rev. **140**, 110755 (2021)
6. Zhou, S., Hu, Z., Gu, W., et al.: Artificial intelligence based smart energy community management: a reinforcement learning approach. CSEE J. Power Energy Syst. **5**(1), 1–10 (2019)

7. Cheng, L., Yu, T.: A new generation of AI: a review and perspective on machine learning technologies applied to smart energy and electric power systems. Int. J. Energy Res. **43**(6), 1928–1973 (2019)

8. Ji, X., Zhang, Y., Mirza, N., et al.: The impact of carbon neutrality on the investment performance: evidence from the equity mutual funds in BRICS. J. Environ. Manage. **297**, 113228 (2021)

9. Chen, S., Liu, J., Zhang, Q., et al.: A critical review on deployment planning and risk analysis of carbon capture, utilization, and storage (CCUS) toward carbon neutrality. Renew. Sustain. Energy Rev. **167**, 112537 (2022)

10. Wang, Y., Li, R., Dong, H., et al.: Capacity planning and optimization of business park-level integrated energy system based on investment constraints. Energy **189**, 116345 (2019)

11. Morariu, C., Morariu, O., Răileanu, S., et al.: Machine learning for predictive scheduling and resource allocation in large scale manufacturing systems. Comput. Ind. **120**, 103244 (2020)

12. Babu, K.E.K.: Artificial intelligence in Bangladesh, its applications in different sectors and relevant challenges for the government: an analysis. Int. J. Public Law Policy **7**(4), 319–333 (2021)

13. Yang, P., Zhang, L., Tao, G.: Smart chemical industry parks in China: current status, challenges, and pathways for future sustainable development. J. Loss Prev. Process Ind. **83**, 105105 (2023)

Research on the Construction of Education Evaluation Model Based on Big Data

Feng Su, Jian Zhang, and Qing Gao[⊠]

Shandong Vocational College of Information Technology, No. 7494, Dongfeng East Street, Weifang City 261041, China
750166578@qq.com

Abstract. In view of the traditional teaching behavior with examination as the core of education evaluation, it is difficult to objectively and fairly evaluate students' learning effectiveness and development potential. Combining the development of data analysis technology and learning science, this paper aims to try to build a teaching evaluation model based on Big data technology with multiple functions of data collection, data mining analysis and data analysis results visualization. Provide reference and basis for decision-makers, and enrich the research path of intelligent teaching evaluation.

Keywords: Big data · Data mining · evaluation model

1 Introduction

The "New Generation Artificial Intelligence Development Plan" points out that by 2025, positive progress will be made in the construction of an intelligent society, providing personalized, diversified, and high-quality basic education services to the public. Education needs to develop, and evaluation is the key. Education evaluation is an important engine for promoting the reform of talent cultivation models and educational innovation, and is also the core link in implementing the fundamental task of cultivating morality and talents in the field of basic education.

However, the traditional education evaluation is based on the teaching behavior with examination as the core, which is difficult to objectively and impartially evaluate students' learning effectiveness and development potential. At present, many scholars are committed to the research on Educational assessment subject, system, strategy, etc., but the research on intelligent teaching evaluation using Big data technology is still quite scarce, so this paper applies Big data technology to teaching evaluation, Analyze the data that may appear in the teaching process, build an intelligent teaching evaluation model based on Big data technology, innovate and develop the traditional education evaluation, improve the education evaluation process and methods, improve the digital and intelligent level of education evaluation, realize scientific, objective and efficient evaluation and feedback, and promote the reform and development of education.

S. He et al. (Eds.): METAVERSE 2023, LNCS 14210, pp. 71–83, 2023.
https://doi.org/10.1007/978-3-031-44754-9_6

2 Model Construction

The teaching evaluation model based on Big data technology mainly consists of three parts. The first part is the acquisition of intelligent teaching Big data. Based on the CIPP evaluation model, an intelligent teaching evaluation system is designed. Through the IOT perception technology, wearable device technology, video monitoring technology, online evaluation and online reading technology and other technologies, the evaluation data is collected in a full process, all-round and multi-dimensional manner, changing the way of manual collection and recording in the past, achieving three-dimensional acquisition of evaluation data, and preprocessing and storage of intelligent teaching Big data. The second part is the mining and analysis of Big data for smart teaching. In information processing and knowledge building, Natural language processing, Knowledge representation and reasoning, data analysis, data mining and other technologies are used to achieve the unified processing and analysis of the acquired data, and to mine the potential laws and values of data. The third part is the visualization of Big data analysis results of intelligent teaching. Through voice interaction, somatosensory interaction, Data and information visualization and other technologies, the results are fed back to users in the form of visualization. The intelligent teaching evaluation model based on Big data technology is shown in Fig. 1.

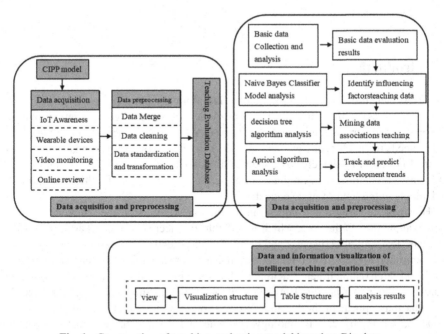

Fig. 1. Construction of teaching evaluation model based on Big data.

2.1 Data Acquisition and Preprocessing

The CIPP evaluation model is a theoretical model for educational evaluation, which includes four parts: background, input, process, and product. It is called a decision oriented or improvement oriented evaluation model. Due to its operability and effectiveness, it is applicable to the entire education system. This article draws inspiration from the CIPP model and combines the connotation of intelligent teaching evaluation. It evaluates the entire teaching process from four aspects: background evaluation, input evaluation, process evaluation, and result evaluation. It designs a multidimensional and three-dimensional online data collection model that covers multiple aspects such as construction level, application level, teaching effectiveness, resource use, personalized support, academic level, student ability, and teacher level.

By utilizing IoT sensing technology, wearable device technology, video surveillance technology, and online review technology, the evaluation data is collected in a comprehensive, multi-dimensional and multi-dimensional manner throughout the entire process, achieving three-dimensional acquisition of evaluation data. Specifically, it includes relying on data collection platforms and equipment to automatically record the various data generated by the evaluation object throughout the entire activity, transforming from "intermittent recording" in the past to "full process recording"; Breaking the boundaries of time and space is not only limited to traditional classrooms, but also includes the acquisition of E-learning data, outdoor teaching activity data, etc.; Multidimensional data refers to the collection of more diverse and comprehensive types of data, including behavioral data, emotional data, physical fitness data, management data, etc. Utilize distributed storage to classify and store the collected data. After comprehensively collecting teaching data, use Big data technology to carry out pre-processing operations such as data consolidation, cleaning, standardization and transformation, find the correlation and mapping correspondence between evaluation objectives and data, eliminate "noise data", screen and integrate valuable data, and form a teaching theme database.

2.2 Data Mining and Analysis

Data mining and analysis is to mine and analyze the massive data generated in the process of intelligent teaching evaluation, and conduct a scientific and comprehensive evaluation of the teaching process. This is the most critical part of the whole process of applying Big data technology to intelligent teaching evaluation. The commonly used analysis methods in data mining mainly include classification, clustering, valuation, prediction, association rules, visualization, etc. From the perspective of the mathematical foundation on which data mining algorithms rely, they are currently mainly divided into three categories: machine learning methods, statistical methods, and neural network methods. Machine learning methods include decision tree, case-based learning, Rule induction and genetic algorithm; Statistical methods can be subdivided into regression analysis, time series analysis, association analysis, cluster analysis, Fuzzy set, rough set, exploratory analysis, support vector machine and nearest neighbor analysis; Neural network methods are divided into forward neural networks, self-organizing neural networks, perceptrons, multi-layer neural networks, deep learning, etc. Based on a deep understanding of data mining algorithms and preprocessing of teaching data, this article first evaluates the collected data based on an intelligent teaching indicator system. Then, various algorithms are used to conduct targeted mining and analysis of the data generated during the teaching process.

2.3 Visualization of Data Analysis Results

Big data visual analysis refers to "using the user interface supporting Information visualization and human-computer interaction methods and technologies supporting the analysis process while automatically analyzing and mining Big data to effectively integrate the computing ability of computers and human cognitive ability to gain insight into large-scale complex data sets [1]. The results of data mining and analysis are generally presented through Data and information visualization. Through visualization, we can more intuitively identify the answers to the questions we seek, identify the relationships, trends, and biases hidden in various intersecting data, and discover the knowledge and patterns hidden in the data. Visual analysis involves meaning construction, human-computer interaction analysis, distributed cognition and other cognitive theories. It plays a particularly important role in Big data analysis, and is especially suitable for complex data mining fields. The visualization technologies applied in Big data analysis mainly include text visualization, network (graph) visualization, spatio-temporal Data and information visualization, multi-dimensional Data and information visualization, etc. There are a large number of software tools that focus on different visualization purposes that have been launched, and they are developing towards a better user experience. Generally speaking, Line chart, bar chart, pie chart, bubble chart and radar chart are often used, which are clear and understandable.

3   Design of Teaching Quality Evaluation System Based on Big Data

3.1   Establishment of Teaching Quality Evaluation Index System

The teaching evaluation indicators must objectively and accurately reflect the basic situation of school education, and the evaluation indicators must be practical, scientific, complete, and easy to operate. This article is based on the CIPP model and combines the connotation of intelligent teaching evaluation. It evaluates the entire teaching process from the perspectives of background evaluation, input evaluation, process evaluation, and result evaluation. The evaluation indicators are composed of a combination of primary and secondary indicators. The primary indicators include four parts: background evaluation, input evaluation, process evaluation, and result evaluation. The secondary indicators include teaching objectives, teaching concepts, teacher strength Resource investment, organizational guarantee, teaching methods, teaching content, student performance, and social recognition. The evaluation of teaching quality is completed through the above 9 indicators, as shown in Table 1.

In order to overcome the interference of human factors, this article adopts Bayesian classification technology to calculate the weight of the established evaluation system. A Bayesian network is a triple (V, E, P), where $V = \{v_1, v_2, ..., v_n)$ is a set of nodes, $E = \{v_iv_j \mid v_i \neq v_j, v_j \in V\}$ $P = \{P(v_i \mid parents(v_i))\}$ is a set of Conditional probability and

Table 1. Evaluation Indicators of Teaching Quality.

Primary indicators	Secondary indicators	Indicator Description
Background evaluation (B1)	Teaching objectives(C1)	It can guide the direction of teaching, stimulate teachers and students, and regulate and control the teaching process
	Teaching philosophy(C2)	Being student-centered, able to pay attention to students' progress and development, and stimulate their interest in learning
Input evaluation(B2)	Teachers(C3)	The teaching staff have appropriate teaching experience and educational background, and can meet teaching requirements
	Resource investment(C4)	The teaching platform is highly advanced and can meet the teaching needs
	organizational guarantee(C5)	Teachers have good adaptability, orderly teaching process and perfect safety measures
Process Evaluation(B3)	teaching method(C6)	Proper use of teaching methods, accurate and standardized explanations and demonstrations; Emphasize ability development
	Teaching content(C7)	Emphasize education on key and difficult points, and allocate learning and training time reasonably
Result evaluation(B4)	Student Achievements(C8)	The students' scores meet the Normal distribution, and the scores of each stage are reasonable
	Social recognition(C9)	High social recognition

a set of Conditional probability functions for each node. The joint probability function of a Bayesian network is represented as follows:

$$P(v_1, v_2, ..., v_n) = \prod_{i=1}^{n} P(v_i|parents(v_i)) = \prod_{i=1}^{n} P(v_i|parents(v_i)) \frac{P(v_i, parents(v_i,))}{P(parents(v_i))}$$

$$(1)$$

The theoretical basis of Bayesian networks comes from Probability theory. Below are several related concepts.

1) Conditional probability. If A and B are two events and $P(A) > 0$, $P(B|A) = \frac{P(AB)}{P(A)}$ is called the Conditional probability of event B under the condition of P (A) where event A occurs.

2) Bayesian formula. Let Sample space be Ω, A be the event of E, B_1, B_2,..., Bn be a group of events of E, and satisfy: $\sum_{i=1}^{n} B_i = \Omega$, $P(B_i) > 0$, $i = 1, 2, ..., n$, B1, B2,..., Bn are incompatible with each other, then there are:

$$P(B_i|A) = \frac{P(A|B_i)P(B_i)}{\sum_{j=1}^{n} P(A|B_j)P(B_j)} \quad i = 1, 2, ..., n \quad (2)$$

According to the primary and secondary indicators determined in Table 1, the Directed acyclic graph of the teaching quality evaluation model based on Bayesian network is drawn, as shown in Fig. 2.

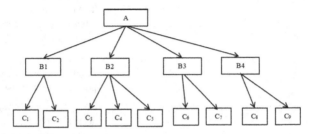

Fig. 2. Directed acyclic graph of teaching quality evaluation model

In the above model, based on the secondary indicators, the evaluation level range $Y = \{y1, y2, y3, y4, y5\}$ is given, representing excellent (95), good (85), average (75), pass (65), and fail (50), respectively. To avoid the influence of human factors, each node represents an event, where the probability of each event occurring is assumed to be equal and the events are independent of each other. In order to determine the impact of various evaluation factors on the evaluation of teaching quality, that is, to determine the probability of the final node and identify the factors that have a significant impact on the results. Assign values to each node based on expert knowledge and actual situation. The probability of an event is calculated based on its occurrence or not, using Eqs. (1) and (2). According to the MSBNX software and method [2], the initial assignment is first given to calculate the probability of the final node, and then the assignment of the evaluation indicators is changed one by one. The assignment of other indicators is restored to the initial state. The impact of the evaluation indicators is determined by comparing the probability of the final node after the change. The comparison results are shown in Table 2.

3.2 Data preparation and preprocessing

Based on the teaching supervision evaluation data of the Academic Affairs Office of our school from 2021 to 2023, association rule analysis is conducted on the professional

Table 2. Weights of various indicators in the teaching quality evaluation system based on bayesian networks

Primary indicators	Weight value
Background evaluation Input evaluation	0.18
Background evaluation Input evaluation	0.19
Process Evaluation	0.31
Result evaluation	0.32

teacher information of the Intelligent Manufacturing Department. The purpose is to explore the correlation between professional teachers' own factors and the evaluation data of supervision, and to use association rule algorithms to uncover implicit and useful relationships. During preprocessing, some data need to be Discretization; In addition, it is necessary to convert the required fields and evaluation scores into A → B format for easy processing; Finally, the association rule mining algorithm is used for computational processing. Assuming the minimum support and minimum confidence based on the specific situation, calculate the support and confidence of each association rule, and finally select the association rules that meet the conditions.

3.3 Comprehensive Evaluation Based on ID3 Algorithm

3.3.1 ID3 Algorithm Clustering

After obtaining survey data, relevant management personnel can obtain comprehensive evaluation results through calculation. There are many commonly used algorithms for data mining, such as genetic algorithm, clustering algorithm, Apriori algorithm, etc. This article combines the characteristics of teaching evaluation and uses the ID3 decision tree method to complete data mining of teaching evaluation. It identifies factors that affect teachers' teaching and provides decision-making basis for teachers to improve their teaching level and quality. Decision trees can purposefully classify a large amount of data to obtain valuable potential information.

As the most typical algorithm in the decision tree algorithm, the ID3 algorithm checks the characteristic attributes of data on nodes at all levels of the decision tree through information gain, selects the attribute with the maximum information gain as the sample partition test attribute, establishes branches according to different values of the attribute, and establishes the nodes and branches at the next level of the decision tree in a recursive manner from each branch instance set, guiding the subset instance to be divided into a certain category. In the ID3 algorithm, let S be the training set and s be the number of samples. Suppose there are m different values for class C_i (i = 1,2..., m), where the number of samples for class C_i is S_i. The expected information required for a given sample classification is:

$$I(s_1, s_2, ...s_m) = -(p_1 \log_2(p_1) + p_2 \log_2(p_2) + ... + p_m \log_2(p_m)) \tag{3}$$

In the above equation, $p_i = {s_i}/{s}$ is the probability that the sample belongs to C_i.

Assuming that there are v different values in attribute A, such as $\{a_1, a_2, ..., a_v\}$, the training set of S is divided into v subsets $\{s_1, s_2, ..., s_v\}$ using attribute A, where the samples of S_j have the same value aj in A. If A is selected as the testing attribute, the classification subset includes multiple branches formed in the S node. Set s_{ij} as the number of C_i like samples in S_j. The expected information entropy of the subset divided by A is:

$$E(A) = \sum_{i=1}^{v} \frac{s_{ij} + ... + s_{mj}}{S} I(s_{ij}, ..., s_{mj}) \qquad (4)$$

where $\frac{s_{ij}+...+s_{mj}}{S}$ is the jth weight value, the encoding information of the branch on the A attribute is obtained as follows:

$$Gain(A) = I(s_{ij}, ..., s_{mj}) - E(A) \qquad (5)$$

Select the attribute with the highest information gain in the algorithm and give it the S test attribute. Create nodes based on the test attribute and label them with attributes, and construct branches based on the attributes for sample partitioning.

3.3.2 Tree Pruning

In the process of creating a decision tree, due to the presence of noise in the training set, there are abnormal branches in the training data. Therefore, it is necessary to prune the decision tree of the noisy branches to solve the problem of some branches being excessively adapted. At present, the most common pruning methods are mainly divided into pre pruning and post pruning techniques. The first pruning method is to directly stop establishing child nodes for branches with exceptions during the process of establishing the decision tree, so as not to form abnormal branches. The post pruning method involves removing some abnormal branches from the decision tree based on the tree building conditions, and rebuilding a new decision tree using leaf nodes.

In this article, based on the classification characteristics of teaching evaluation data, a post pruning method based on the minimum error principle is adopted. After the decision tree is fully generated, the excess branches are pruned and a new decision tree is obtained using leaf nodes. Therefore, by establishing a decision tree to determine any instance, the mining process is shown in Fig. 3.

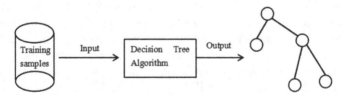

Fig. 3. Decision Tree Mining Process

By using the decision tree algorithm to test the information gain feature attributes, the maximum gain value is obtained to form a decision tree node, ensuring the highest example recognition accuracy while minimizing the number of decision tree nodes. Construct branches based on different feature values, recursively process the subset of branch instances, establish decision tree nodes and branches, until all instances in a subset are the same subset.

3.3.3 ID3 Algorithm Data Mining

Perform decision tree analysis on the four primary indicators established earlier. Assumption K1: Background evaluation; K2: Input evaluation; K3: process evaluation; K4: Result evaluation: Four training sample data were collected, and 10 frontline teachers from the college were organized to evaluate the teaching effectiveness of the course. The evaluation Elo rating system is divided into 5 levels, namely: A excellent (90–100); B: Good (80–90); C: Moderate (70–80); D: Qualified (60–70); E: Unqualified (<60); The teaching quality evaluations obtained from 10 teachers are shown in Table 3.

Table 3. Teaching Quality Evaluation

Teacher ID	Rating indicators				Evaluate Results
	K1	K2	K3	K4	
1	B	B	B	A	Good
2	B	B	B	B	Good
3	B	B	B	B	Good
4	C	C	C	B	Medium
5	B	C	C	C	Medium
6	A	A	A	A	Excellent
7	C	B	C	C	Medium
8	A	A	B	B	Good
9	B	C	B	B	Good
10	B	B	C	C	Good

According to Table 3. The expected information (or information) required for a given sample is:

$$I(S) = -\frac{1}{10}\log_2(\frac{1}{10}) - \frac{6}{10}\log_2(\frac{6}{10}) - \frac{3}{10}\log_2(\frac{3}{10}) = 1.293 \tag{6}$$

For attribute K1:

$$E(S_A) = -\frac{1}{2}\log_2(\frac{1}{2}) - \frac{1}{2}\log_2(\frac{1}{2}) = 1 \tag{7}$$

$$E(S_B) = -\frac{1}{6}\log_2(\frac{1}{6}) - \frac{5}{6}\log_2(\frac{5}{6}) = 0.65 \tag{8}$$

$$E(S_C) = -\frac{2}{2} \log_2(\frac{2}{2}) - 0 = 0 \qquad (9)$$

$$E(K1) = \frac{6}{10} E(S_A) + \frac{2}{10} E(S_B) + \frac{2}{10} E(S_C) = 0.73 \qquad (10)$$

Therefore, the information gain of attribute K1 can be calculated as:

$$Gain(K1) = I(S) - E(K1) = 0.563 \qquad (11)$$

Similarly, it can be calculated that:

$$Gain(K2) = 0.507$$

$$Gain(K3) = 0.689$$

$$Gain(K4) = 0.472$$

From the above, it can be seen that E3 has the greatest information gain. Therefore, E3 attribute is selected as the test attribute of the root node, and corresponding values are branched down at the root node. Continue to recursively call the ID3 method to divide. If the path from the root node to the node already includes all attributes, or if the training samples of the current node belong to the same class, the algorithm ends. The final decision tree generated is shown in Fig. 4.

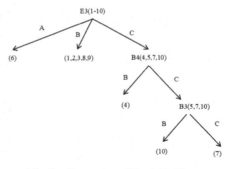

Fig. 4. Generation of Decision Trees

3.3.4 Generate Classification Rules

According to the final decision tree returned by the ID3 algorithm, as shown in Fig. 4, each path from the tree root to the leaf of the decision tree corresponds to the conjunctive of a group of attribute tests, and the decision tree represents the disjunction of these conjunctives. After generating the decision tree, it is convenient to extract the knowledge described by the decision tree and use If_ Then's statement represents the rules. Each path from node to leaf node corresponds to a decision rule.

From Fig. 3–1, there are six nodes and six rules in the decision structure, as follows:

(1) If (E2 = A) then E5 = Excellent;
(2) If (E2 = B) then E5 = Moderate;
(3) If (E2 = C and E4 = B) then E5 = Poor;
(4) If (E2 = C and E4 = C and E3 = C) then E5 = Poor;
(5) If (E2 = C and E4 = C and E3 = B and E1 = B) then E5 = Moderate;
(6) If (E2 = C and E4 = C and E3 = B and E1 = C) then E5 = Poor;

From the above analysis, it can be seen that the E2 indicator is the most important in the system. Teachers with E2 as A or B will receive a final evaluation of medium or excellent; Teachers with E2 as C cannot receive excellence. This indicates that teachers who are recognized by students have the best comprehensive evaluation. Students place more emphasis on the teaching effectiveness during the teaching process, that is, whether they have learned something under the guidance of the teacher. This puts forward higher and updated requirements for our teachers.

3.4   Analysis and Feedback of Association Rule Mining Results

Process evaluation is currently the main factor in teaching evaluation, and these factors have a huge impact on students. Therefore, this article further explores the association rules of the above factors.

Apply data mining technology and Apriori algorithm to mine evaluation data, identify hidden data that has an impact on improving teaching effectiveness, and provide it to school teaching management departments and relevant teachers for learning and reference. Mining corresponding association rules from the selected data source and providing them to users. To provide information services for users to make scientific and accurate decisions, the following types of information can be mined: each type of teacher (classified by educational background, professional title, etc.) has excellent and good teaching characteristics; What characteristics of teachers are closely related to teaching effectiveness. The details are as follows:

(1) Generate frequent itemsets

Utilize mining techniques to identify teacher characteristics with excellent and good teaching outcomes. Firstly, by screening the database, a total of 80 records with a total evaluation score of >=85 were obtained, and a total of 100 records with a total evaluation score of 70.84 were obtained. Set the minimum support and use the Apriori algorithm to find frequent itemsets.

(2) Generate Association Rules

After generating frequent itemsets, based on the algorithm for generating association rules, for any frequent K-itemset, identify all candidate sets as a prerequisite for association rules, and calculate the corresponding confidence level. The results of mining the teaching evaluation data are shown in Tables 4, 5 and 6.

From Table 4, it can be seen that teachers with teaching experience of 10–25 years have a rating of "good", resulting in a higher confidence level. It can be seen that teachers with 10–25 years of teaching experience have rich teaching experience, excellent teaching results, and high recognition of supervision. The impact of teaching experience on teaching effectiveness is obvious. Middle aged teachers have excellent teaching

Table 4. Data Mining Results on Teaching Age

Rule	Standard	Category	Support	Confidence
Teaching experience greater than 25	[90–100]	Excellent	18%	50%
Teaching experience greater than 10 but less than 25	[80–89]	Good	32%	78%
Teaching experience less than 10	[70–79]	Moderate	24%	62%

quality and are the backbone of teaching. Therefore, more attention should be paid to the cultivation of young teachers.

Table 5. Data Mining Results on Academic Degrees

Rule	Standard	Category	Support	Confidence
Master's degree, with teaching experience greater than 10 but less than 25 years	[90–100]	Excellent	34%	79%
Bachelor's degree, with teaching experience greater than 10 but less than 25 years	[80–89]	Good	32%	68%

From Table 5, it can be seen that there is a high correlation between teacher education and teaching evaluation. High education teachers have higher scores in teaching quality evaluation, as there is currently no doctoral degree in the college and the degree is a master's degree with high confidence. This requires schools to increase their efforts in talent introduction, but if there is a high level of support for undergraduate degrees, it may be due to a relatively large proportion of teachers with undergraduate degrees. Schools should take measures to urge teachers to improve their academic qualifications.

Table 6. Data Mining Results on Professional Titles

Rule	Standard	Category	Support	Confidence
Professional title as a professor, with teaching experience greater than 25 years	[90–100]	Excellent	30%	75%
Professional title is Associate Professor, with teaching experience greater than 10 but less than 25 years	[80–89]	Good	35%	82%
Title as a lecturer, with less than 10 years of teaching experience	[70–79]	Moderate	24%	62%

From Table 6, it can be seen that the professional title of a teacher is also highly correlated with the evaluation of teaching. The professional title of an associate professor has a high degree of confidence. Currently, the number of professors in the college is relatively small, and the teaching quality evaluation of associate professor teachers is excellent. Therefore, teachers should be encouraged to continuously strive to promote their professional titles.

4   Conclusion

The evaluation of teaching quality in universities is a complex task, and to do it well, it must rely on real and reliable data. This article is based on the CIPP model and adopts Bayesian classification technology to assign weights to the established evaluation system. Cluster analysis and association rules are applied to explore the relevant associations and their value meanings behind the data. Then, data mining technology and Apriori algorithm are further applied to mine the evaluation data, identifying data hidden in the data that has an impact on improving teaching effectiveness, And provide it for learning and reference from the school's teaching management department and relevant teachers.

References

1. Bangqi, L.: Evaluation of intelligent technology empowered education: connotation, overall framework, and practical path. China's Audiovis. Educ. **4**, 16–24 (2021)
2. Xiaoting, L.: Construction of smart teaching evaluation model based on Big data technology. Scientific and technological innovation and application education (12), 11–19 (2023). Author, F., Author, S., Author, T.: Book title. 2nd edn. Publisher, Location (1999)
3. Dianwei, Z.: Visual analysis of the evolution path, research hotspots, and frontiers of intelligent education evaluation. Ind. Technol. Voc. Educ. **18**(1), 110–114 (2020)
4. Zhang, Q., Yang, L.T., Chen, Z., Li, P.: A survey on deep learning for big data. Informat. Fus. **42**, 146–157 (2018).[5] Wang Yuntao. "new infrastructure" to promote the comprehensive upgrade of artificial intelligence infrastructure. Communications world 2020, No. 835, 22–3
5. Bangqi, L., et al.: Reference framework for regional education big data development. Mod. Educ. Technol. **28**(4), :5–12 (2018)

Short Paper Track

CBDC – An Alternative to Cryptocurrency in the Metaverse: An Indian Perspective

Janhavi Kalal[1] (ID), Bipin Palande[1](✉) (ID), Shreeya Chidambar Rajpurohit[1] (ID),
and Shilpa Parkhi[2] (ID)

[1] School of Economics and Commerce, Dr. Vishwanath Karad MIT World Peace University,
Pune, Maharashtra, India
{1202220068,bipin.palande,shreeya.rajpurohit}@mitwpu.edu.in
[2] Symbiosis Institute of Business Management, Symbiosis International (Deemed University),
Pune, Maharashtra, India
shilpaparkhi@sibmpune.edu.in

Abstract. The purpose of this paper is to understand the link between Meta-verse and the Central Bank Digital Currencies (CBDCs) which are issued by some of the Central Governments around the world. Cryptocurrencies are an integral part of the Metaverse ecosystem. The governments are looking at CBDC as an alternative to fight the Cryptocurrencies, prominently because of the security concerns it has raised in the recent past. The study focuses on the Indian perspective of CBDC (e₹). This study is conducted through a review of the literature published in research papers, newspaper articles, and publications by Indian regulatory authorities. The authors have also included their observations from using the CBDC App launched by one of the leading commercial banks in India. The study tries to find a link between Metaverse and CBDC via Cryptocurrency. Since CBDC is still in its pilot stage in India, it is to be seen as to how successful it is in the Indian financial system. Further studies can be conducted at a later stage when and if India's central bank (the Reserve Bank of India) takes CBDC to its full implementation stage.

Keywords: Metaverse · Cryptocurrency · Central Bank Digital Currency
(CBDC) · eRupee (e₹) · Reserve Bank of India (RBI)

1 Introduction

The web was developed by Tim Berners-Lee in Switzerland [12]. Web 1.0 (Static Web) is the first generation of web, which according to Berners-Lee was potentially regarded as a read-only web as well as a system of cognition, which only allowed to search and read information. Web 2.0 (Interactive Web) was coined by Tim Berners as a read-write web. It can contribute information and relate with other internet users, which has significantly altered the web's environment in a short period. Now with more advancements, we are transitioning towards Web 3.0 (Semantic Web) where a decentralized internet system will work and have its applications using cryptocurrency. It brings emphasis to the internet infrastructure that enables users to accomplish anything they want without relying on any firm or government [11].

Metaverse

The concept of the Metaverse is not new. Although, it was initially presented in Neal

S. He et al. (Eds.): METAVERSE 2023, LNCS 14210, pp. 87–97, 2023.
https://doi.org/10.1007/978-3-031-44754-9_7

Stephenson's 1992 dystopian science fiction novel "Snow Crash", it was originally described and popularised as "cyberspace" in William Gibson's 1984 science fiction novel "Neuromancer" [17]. "The Metaverse is the post-reality universe, a perpetual and persistent multiuser environment merging physical reality with digital virtuality" [20]. It can also be defined as a computer-generated other reality in which individuals may exchange and interact as if they were in the actual world. The metaverse is now a virtual space in which individuals engage socially and economically by utilizing avatars (virtual representations) without being restricted by real-world limitations such as time and location [2]. As the emerging concept of the next-generation Internet, Metaverse intends to create a completely immersive, highly spatiotemporal, and self-sustaining virtual shared place for people to play, work, and socialize. Metaverse is transitioning from science fiction to a future reality, due to recent developments in developing technologies such as extended reality, artificial intelligence, and blockchain [35].

Metaverse and Its Applications

Metaverse is an evolving area of research. Ongoing newer research is contributing to the applications of Metaverse. However, the following are some of its major applications:

a) Games: It is the most popular Metaverse application right now. Games are an excellent way to explore the Metaverse due to their technological maturity, user pairing, and content flexibility. Examples: Fortnite, Second Life, Roblox, etc. are the prominent ones [35].
b) Social Experience: Metaverse has the potential to transform our society by allowing a variety of immersive social applications such as virtual lifestyles, virtual commerce, virtual dating, virtual chatting, across-the-globe travel, as well as space/time travel [35].
c) Online Collaboration: Metaverse offers up exciting possibilities for immersive virtual collaboration, such as telecommuting in virtual workplaces, studying and learning in virtual schools, and group chats and conferences in virtual conference rooms [35].

What Role Do Cryptocurrencies Play in the Metaverse?

As the metaverse has its foundation in blockchain, so do cryptocurrencies as well, hence it will be the most widely used method of payment in the metaverse. Using cryptocurrency will be the most straightforward, practical, and cost-effective way to start a worldwide metaverse shopping experience. One may use digital currency at any retailer, regardless of location. When one uses crypto, he/she saves money on international communication and transaction charges, and most merchants in the metaverse accept a variety of cryptocurrencies [18]. In Metaverse, cryptocurrencies are divided into two broad categories "coins" & "tokens". Metaverse coin is more frequently traded and can be purchased or sold in exchange for other cryptocurrencies or fiat money. The Metaverse token can only be exchanged for other cryptocurrencies.

Transactions in Metaverse are carried out with the help of various cryptocurrencies, to name a few; MANA, SAND and AXS, and SLP. These currencies are used in multiple parallels such as digital real estate, gaming universe, etc. [2, 32]. The stock market performance of 43 firms mainly Bitcoin and cryptocurrency companies saw significant price rises during the COVID-19 era. As a consequence, the authors concluded that price bubbles are persistent [16]. Since cryptocurrencies are regarded as the most volatile digital currencies and as per the analysis done over cryptocurrencies in Metaverse, developers should examine appropriate alternatives that provide the multiverse with trustworthy virtual currencies along with methods that could reduce the excessive volatility. A similar option to use permissioned blockchains to build a restricted metaverse can be used wherein a central authority may govern the virtual economy, ensuring system stability and reducing market speculation [34]. Central Bank Digital Currency (CBDC) can be one such alternative, which the authors have presented in much detail in further sections.

2 Digital Currency: An Overview

Friends & Family are something which one cannot buy, for everything else Money is required! If one wants to possess a tangible or even intangible thing, one needs an exchange for it. 'Money' serves this purpose. The definition of Money has been evolving for ages; however, it means the same for everyone even today. Money is anything that is used as a medium of exchange, a store of value, and for repayment of loans or debts. It took a long process for money to be what it is today. Earlier there was no money, instead, the Barter Exchange of goods and services was in use. The concept of money evolved with metals such as Gold, Copper being used as money, which were then minted into Coins. Later, paper money came into use followed by plastic money in the form of debit & credit cards. The evolution journey continued with electronic money (SWIFT, Internet Banking, etc.) coming into the picture. Today, the financial system has advanced to digital money (digital wallets, etc.) which is also known as the most used form of money besides cash. The latest in the series is a digital currency with the development of cryptos [9, 15]. As digital currencies are not available in the physical form and will be transacted in digital or electronic form only, it's been considered a revolutionary form of money. According to the report by European Central Bank, digital currencies can be categorized into two – regulated (by authorities) and the other one is unregulated (not controlled by any legal authorities) [8]. Someone whose identity is unknown to the world must be handling the backend operations of unregulated digital currencies but there is no governmental authority as such that governs the operations like generation, distribution, and monitoring of currency.

Digital currency came into existence after the 'Global Financial Crisis of 2008' due to the economic turndown of the banking giants – Bear Stearns and Lehman Brothers went bankrupt [36]. Most of the world went through a massive financial shock with job loss, distressed asset sale, and withdrawal of holdings; which resulted in a loss of public trust in financial systems, ultimately resulting in the general public looking for a better alternative [1]. The digital currency was first proposed by a person with the pseudonym Satoshi Nakamoto back in 2009 and became operational in 2010. The first digital currency created was Bitcoin [4]. Cryptographic proof was the base of Bitcoin at the time of introduction, unlike normal currencies which are issued based on trust. This facilitated the transaction between two parties without any intervention of a third party [21].

3 Working of Cryptocurrency

Blockchain technology, which is based on cryptography, is how cryptocurrency functions. To accomplish the goal of sharing the information with just designated parties, this technology protects the information and communicates through codes. This keeps the information safe from unauthorized access. 'Crypt' in the word 'Cryptography' means 'concealed', while 'graphy' is 'writing' [28]. Using Distributed Ledger Technology (DLT), information is stored in groups on several computer networks in the case of Blockchain. Each block has a limited amount of storage space for data; once it is full, the data is secured via cryptography and cannot be readily changed, erased, or damaged. After that, all of these blocks are linked together to form the so-called blockchain. [13]. The central bank-issued currency notes are represented digitally by CBDC. In other terms, it is a technological representation of anything (in this case, fiat/physical currency in the form of digital data. CBDC is a novel form of central bank money that differs from physical currency or central bank reserve/settlement accounts, according to a report by the Reserve Bank of India [10]. It is a Central Bank liability that is valued in an active unit of account. CBDC works as a store of value and a medium of exchange.

4   Comparison: Regulated and Unregulated Digital Currency

Post the subprime crisis of 2008, the financial systems were facing a distressed state. Users of the system needed an alternative to the system which resulted in the emergence of cryptos. According to Nakamato's white paper on Bitcoin [21], bitcoin eliminated the issue of traditional financial structure. To mention a few: the system is decentralized i.e. it has a peer-to-peer network that does not need any central authority to validate the transactions. It provides a secure network due to the use of cryptographic techniques to store information. Cryptocurrency transactions are much faster and cheaper in comparison with traditional payment mechanisms. It facilitates cross-border payments leading to its universal access across the globe. Due to the anonymity of the transaction within the network, it ensures a very high level of privacy [15].

In addition to being a sort of investment or store of value where one earns interest on assets, cryptocurrencies are utilized as a medium of trade. Digital Currency being a newer area, it becomes challenging to comprehend how the market operates, which reduces trading efficiency. The volatility of cryptocurrency values further prevents widespread adoption and usage. When trading or exchanging cryptocurrencies online, network issues could cause the transaction to fail or go slowly, making it impossible to recover any lost cryptocurrency. Another issue with cryptocurrencies is that they are entirely online, which is again vulnerable to scams and hacks because they are still in their infancy. Additionally, because of its anonymity, various anti-social acts like money laundering and funding for terrorism can be supported and promoted, which is bad for economies all over the world [38]. Regulated digital currencies have developed as a safe and secure alternative to uncontrolled digital currencies in light of all their disadvantages. Because regulated cryptocurrencies are centralized, that is, issued by central banks, and do not operate on peer-to-peer networks, they make it easier for authorities to properly oversee the system. Since CBDC is a form of official currency issued by the government, using it is simple and requires no prior market knowledge. CBDC will currently use the internet to assist on-time transfers, but central banks are also working on offline transfer options. The issuance of CBDC will assist central banks all over the world in reducing the costs associated with producing and maintaining real coins and currency notes. Because even those without bank accounts can access CBDC, it will help increase financial inclusion. Since CBDC does not offer an offline payment alternative as yet, a few difficulties like internet and security, etc. also arise because the technology being employed is still in its infancy and is prone to cyber-attacks. [37, 38].

Below is a comparison of the different payment options presented in Table 1 [29]

Table 1. A comparison of various modes of payment

Parameters	Fiat/ Physical currency	Cryptos (Unregulated)	CBDC (Regulated)	Mobile money (UPI, RTGS, NEFT)
Overview	It comprises coins and paper notes	Cryptocurrency is an encrypted data string that denotes a unit of money	CBDCs are digital versions of cash that are issued and regulated by central banks	It refers to the payment made using mobile which is linked to the bank accounts
Tangibility, portability & durability	It is tangible, portable, and durable	It is not tangible as it is stored in cyberspace, However, it is portable and durable	It is not tangible as it is stored in cyberspace, however, it is portable and durable	It is portable
Uniformity, acceptability & facilitates a medium of exchange	It is uniform throughout the economy and has a general acceptance. Due to its general acceptance, it is used as a medium of exchange	Cryptocurrency is also uniform. It is still in an early stage and lacks acceptance from economies throughout the world and hence is not widely used as an exchange medium	CBDC is also uniform. And is facing the same problem as crypto in its acceptance and usage	Since one uses the money available in their bank accounts which is legal tender, it is uniform
Volatility	It is not at all volatile	Cryptocurrencies are volatile by design	CBDCs are more secure & inherently not volatile	Mobile money is not volatile
Store of value & liquidity	It acts as a store of value and is highly liquid due to its readily accessible nature	Cryptos are also liquid and provide a store of value	Even CBDC is liquid and acts as a store of value	Mobile money facilitates as the store of value and liquidity
Settlement time	Instantaneous	Sometimes instantaneous as it takes time for every block to form	Instantaneous	It seems that funds are transferred but they are not moved, it takes time for interbank settlements

4.1   Indian Regulators and the Crypto World

India is a vastly spread geography with a market of around 140 billion people today. This attracts both the good and bad of the world to India. The businesses look at it as a huge market for selling their goods and services. However, on the other hand, there also runs a risk of the quick spread of some technology which may create a nuisance in the economy by quickly spreading the ill effects of the product. Cryptocurrency caught the attention of economies around the world in 2013. A report published by RBI has summarised how RBI, the apex bank of India, was always skeptical and critical of cryptocurrency [3]. It was first in 2013 when RBI took cognizance of the virtual currencies in its Financial Stability Report [23]. RBI then cautioned the users about the risk of the virtual currency framework through its first press [24]. These press releases highlighted the fact that the creation, trading, or usage of virtual currencies was not backed by any authority and the participants carrying out these activities too are unregistered. In 2015, it also questioned the very existence of cryptos because of their anonymous nature as it went against the global money laundering rules [25]. In 2016, RBI raised issues concerning data security and consumer protection and its impact on monetary policy's effectiveness, when talking about virtual currencies and P2P lending [26]. This was followed by the government which formed an inter-disciplinary committee of multiple ministries of the government along with RBI, the State Bank of India (SBI), and NITI Aayog in 2017 to check the then status of governing virtual currencies' regulatory framework [19]. This committee submitted its report to the government. The finance minister Nirmala Sitharaman emphasized that she was waiting for the cabinet to approve the bill on cryptocurrency [33]. Simultaneously, court battles between the parties supporting the cryptos and the regulators were going on. RBI could survive multiple arguments challenging its authority to regulate / ban cryptos which were upheld by The Supreme Court [3]. In 2022, the Indian government brought cryptocurrencies under the purview of taxation laws. It named the cryptos as 'Virtual Digital Assets' which included cryptocurrencies and non-fungible tokens (NFTs). The gains made on the sale of these assets will be taxed at 30%. Neither the basic exemption limit nor any expenditure except the cost of acquisition would not be applicable for this type of income. It would also attract TDS @1% subject to certain conditions [5]. As of Jan 2023, the government authorities had seized assets worth Rs. 936 crores (~$115 mn) under Prevention of Money Laundering and worth Rs. 289 crores (~$35 mn) under Foreign Exchange Management [22]. Now, it is evident that the Indian authorities are not in favour of accepting cryptocurrencies as legal tender anytime soon. However, looking at the popularity of digital currencies around the world and in India too, they decided to come up with a regulated digital currency in the form of a CBDC. Detailed information about e-Rupee, the digital currency of India is presented in the next section.

5   e₹- The Indian CBDC

Finance Minister Nirmala Sitharaman in her Budget 2022–23 speech proposed for the first time, the issue of CBDC by the Reserve Bank of India (RBI) in the financial year 2022–23. It will be a boost for the digital economy. It will help the currency management system [7]. The concept note released by RBI in February 2021 focuses on creating awareness about CBDC and its planned features [24]. Digital currency which will be as close as possible to paper currency and effortlessly managing the process were the two basic considerations of RBI. Possible uses of the digital rupee, issuance mechanisms, technology, and design choices were the key considerations [7]. On 1st November 2022, Digital Rupee– Wholesale (e₹-W) was launched in the pilot Wholesale segment to make the interbank market more efficient. Whereas Digital Rupee – Retails (e₹-R) was launched on 1st December 2022 in the retail segment within a closed user group (CUG) that comprises participating customers and merchants [14].

5.1 How will it Work?

Eight banks have been identified by RBI for phase-wise participation in the retail pilot project. The State Bank of India, the ICICI Bank, the Yes Bank, and the IDFC First Bank are the initial 4 banks. This pilot will run in 4 major cities – Mumbai, Delhi, Bengaluru, and Bhuvaneshwar. In the later stage, the Union Bank of India, the Kotak Mahindra Bank, the HDFC bank, and The Bank of Baroda will participate in the retail project subsequently extending to Ahmedabad, Gangtok, Guwahati, Hyderabad, Indore, Kochi, Lucknow, Patna, and Shimla cities. RBI launched the pilot retail version of CBDC on 1st December 2022. The e₹-R represents legal tender being in the form of a Digital token i.e. electronic version of cash [14].

5.2 Benefits of Digital Currency to the Indian Economy

- Faster payments systems
- Efficient Currency Management Options
- Lead to disintermediation in the banking sector.
- Moving its cash-intensive transaction preferences toward CBDC
- Reduction in the cost of storage, printing, and transportation of cash
- A less volatile digital asset [27]

5.3 Implementation

a. **Banks' process**

   The customer must be the account holder of the bank. Banks have selected a few individual and merchant account holders for the pilot. The digital rupee will be accessible to the customers through e-wallets made available by the banks once they receive the necessary consent from the customer. The required amount of money would be converted to CBDC as per the customer's preference and transferred to the wallet from the linked Bank Account. Customers will not be charged for this conversion of the rupee into CBDC and vice-versa [10].

b. **Customers' process**

   The customers are required to download the app, register and verify their sim and open a digital wallet on their phones. Then, they will link the wallet to their bank account by entering Debit card details via the app. After the bank account is linked to the e-wallet, transfer of money from the bank account to the digital wallet is possible. And now, they can perform money transactions between the wallets of different users.

Transactions may happen among select customers and merchants through QR codes as well as through phone numbers [30]. This pilot is being carried out to verify the overall resilience of the procedure. Other banks will be participating in the usage of e-wallets based on their learnings, experiences, and comments [27]. Every bank is expected to provide at least 10,000 clients or merchants to guarantee an acceptable sample base test, which will provide the RBI with useful data to work with [31].

The Advantage of CBDC Over Unified Payment Interface (UPI)

CBDC offers one benefit over the UPI, which is arguably the most often utilised mechanism of the payment transaction, in that no audit trail is left behind. When a consumer uses UPI to make a payment, it is a bank-to-bank transfer, so banks know how much they are paying and to whom. Each transaction generates an audit trail. CBDC, on the other hand, is like currency in the wallet. Banks will never know who has paid whom or how much has been paid.

Current Scenarios in CBDC Space

In the next phase after the launch of CBDC in a pilot stage, RBI plans to expand ongoing pilots in CBDC-Retail and CBDC-Wholesale in the year 2023-24. Five more banks viz. Punjab National Bank, Canara Bank, Federal Bank, Axis Bank, and IndusInd Bank, have been added to the pilot [6]. Axis Bank has launched Axis Bank Digital Rupee App for users to experience the world of the digital rupee and to have convenient, safe, and secure Digital Currency transactions under the regulatory supervision of RBI (Fig. 1).

Fig. 1. Sample Digital Currency. (Image Source: https://www.axisbank.com/digital-rupee-cbdc/?cta=megamenu-retail-DigitalRupee)

First-Hand User Experience

The pilot stage is still going on as of August 2023, there is not much data published on the user experience of the e₹ App. The authors had access to one of the banks currently in the pilot stage and were able to transact using e-Rupee (CBDC). They were able to experience the user interface of the application. The authors downloaded the mobile application named "Axis Mobile Digital Rupee" from the Play Store and loaded the amount from their respective bank accounts into digital wallets. The denominations available on the application were 50 paise, 1 rupee, 10 rupees, 20 rupees, 50 rupees, 100 rupees, and 500 rupees. A transfer transaction was carried out between authors wherein it was noticed that in case of amounts other than the denominations available in the wallet, the working was similar to that of physical cash where the change (balance amount) is credited to the sender. The denominations credited as a change may be configured by the system as per the availability of the denominations (Fig. 2).

Fig. 2. Screenshots taken by authors from "Axis Mobile Digital Rupee" App

6 Conclusions

Metaverse is the virtual world created with the help of technology. Metaverse is built on the technological bases of Virtual as well as Augmented Reality, the Internet of Things, Blockchain, and Artificial Intelligence. One can experience different services virtually like gaming, tourism, education, real estate, etc. by seating at a comfortable remote location of their own choice. This has enhanced the user experience for these services. However, these services are not free and come at a cost, which currently is settled through Cryptocurrencies, which are also built on Blockchain technology. However, many governmental authorities all over the world are concerned about the popularity of Cryptocurrencies in their respective national economies due to their security concerns. Due to the way Cryptos are built, there is no control over their usage, circulation, and management. Hence, Cryptos may be used by miscreants to various undesirable activities including disrupting the economy, creating a parallel economy, terror funding, etc. This gave rise to the idea of having a digital currency built on the same technology, having the same set of benefits but which can be under the control of the government. Total 11 countries (as of July 2023) have so far issued their versions of CBDCs. India launched its CBDC (e₹) in the year 2022. The currency is issued by its central bank – The Reserve Bank of India under the supervision of the Ministry of Finance. Currently, 9 banks (as of July 2023) have been included in the pilot stage. The CBDC can be accessed and transacted through the App. The success of the Digital Currency initiative depends upon its acceptance by the users, both retail and wholesale. How successful it will be, only time will tell. Till that time, governments would be on the lookout for minimizing the ill effects of Cryptocurrencies on the economy.

Acknowledgments. The authors are grateful to Dr. Ramdas Gambhir, (Professor Emeritus, Department of Public Policy, Dr. Vishwanath Karad MIT World Peace University, Pune, India), and Dr. Anand J Kulkarni (Professor & Associate Director Institute of Artificial Intelligence AI, Dr. Vishwanath Karad MIT World Peace University, Pune, India) for reading through manuscripts and providing insights into writing the article.

References

1. Rejeb, A., Rejeb, K., Keogh, J.G.: Cryptocurrencies in modern finance: a literature review. Etikonomi **20**(1), 93–118 (2021). https://doi.org/10.15408/etk.v20i1.16911
2. Akkus, H.T., Gursoy, S., Dogan, M., Demir, A.B.: Metaverse and metaverse cryptocurrencies (meta coins): bubbles or future. Pressacademia **9**, 22–29 (2022). https://doi.org/10.17261/Pressacademia.2022.1542
3. Arora, G.: RBI and the Indian Crypto Industry. SSRN Electr. J. (2020)
4. Bissessar, S.: Opportunities and risks associated with the advent of digital currency in the Caribbean. ECLAC, United Nations, Santiago, Chile (2016)
5. Buddhadev, N.: Decoding crypto taxation as per budget 2022–23. Livemint: https://www.livemint.com/money/personal-finance/decoding-crypto-taxation-as-per-budget-202223-11644166917586.html (2022)
6. Das, B.: https://www.businesstoday.in/: https://www.businesstoday.in/latest/policy/story/rbi-says-it-would-expand-e-rupee-pilot-to-include-more-banks-locations-in-fy24-383421-2023-05-30 (2023)
7. Economic Times. https://economictimes.indiatimes.com/tech/technology/budget-2022-india-to-get-its-own-digital-currency-by-rbi-next-year-says-fm/articleshow/89268178.cms?from=mdr (2022)
8. European Central Bank: Continuity and change – how the challenges of today prepare the ground for tomorrow. Frankfurt: European Central Bank (2022)
9. Evolution of Currency in Hindi (2022)
10. FinTech Department, RBI: Concept Note on Central Bank Digital Currency. FinTech Department, Reserve Bank of India (2022)
11. Getting, B.: Basic Definitions. Practical Ecommerce: https://www.practicalecommerce.com/Basic-Definitions-Web-1-0-Web-2-0-Web-3-0 (2007)
12. Gonzales, D.: Metaverse Investing: How NFTs Web 3.0. Virtual Land and Virtual Reality Are Going to Change the World as We Know it (2021)
13. Hayes, A.: Blockchain Facts: What Is It, How It Works, and How It Can Be Used. Retrieved from Investopedia: https://www.investopedia.com/terms/b/blockchain.asp (2022)
14. India launches digital rupee pilot project: what is it and how will it work? The Indian Express: https://indianexpress.com/article/explained/explained-economics/digital-rupee-pilot-project-launching-on-december-1-what-is-it-and-how-will-it-work-8296610/ (2022)
15. Investopedia: Digital Currency Types, Characteristics, Pros & Cons, Future Uses. Retrieved from Investopedia: https://www.investopedia.com/terms/d/digital-currency.asp (2022)
16. Jalan, A., Matkovskyy, R., Valerio, P.: Shall the winning last? A study of recent bubbles and persistence. Financ. Res. Lett. **45**, 102162 (2021)
17. Kose, M.: What Is the Metaverse and Why Is It So Important? Can We Move Our Lives to a Digital Universe? In: Bakirci, C.M. (ed.), The Evolutionary Tree: https://evrimagaci.org/metaverse-nedir-ve-neden-cok-onemlidir-yasamlarimizi-dijital-bir-evrene-tasiyabilir-miyiz-11135 (2021). Retrieved 30 Jul 2023
18. Laeeq, D.K.: Metaverse: Why, How and What (n.d.).
19. Mishra, A.R.: Govt forms panel to study virtual currencies framework. Livemint: https://www.livemint.com/Industry/zjn9Czn5mo5r9212sLAxWP/Govt-forms-panel-to-study-virtual-currencies-framework.html (2017)
20. Mystakidis, S.: Metaverse. Encyclopedia **2**(1), 486–497 (2022). https://doi.org/10.3390/encyclopedia2010031
21. Nakamoto, S.: Bitcoin: A Peer-to-Peer Electronic Cash System (2008)
22. PIB: Crypto Assets are borderless, and require international collaboration to prevent regulatory arbitrage. Press Information Bureau, Government of India. https://pib.gov.in/PressReleseDetailm.aspx?PRID=1896722 (2023)

23. RBI: Financial Stability Report. The RBI, Mumbai (2013)
24. RBI: RBI Press Releases. Retrieved from Reserve Bank of India: https://rbidocs.rbi.org.in/rdocs/PressRelease/PDFs/IEPR1261VC1213.PDF (2013)
25. RBI: Financial Stability Report. The RBI, Mumbai (2015)
26. RBI: Financial Stability Report. The RBI, Mumbai (2016)
27. Reserve Bank of India: https://pib.gov.in/PressReleasePage.aspx?PRID=1882883 (2023)
28. Richards, K.: cryptocurrency. Tech-target: https://www.techtarget.com/searchsecurity/definition/cryptography#:~:text=The%20word%20%22cryptography%22%20is%20derived,the%20Egyptian%20practice%20of%20hieroglyphics (2021)
29. Sattath, 2022 Sattath, I.H.: Revisiting the Properties of Money. The European Money and Finance Forum, 6 (2022)
30. State Bank of India: FAQ's. https://sbi.co.in/web/personal-banking/cards/debit-card/faq-on-cbdc#:~:text=List%20of%20your%20connected%20State,expiry%20of%20your%20debit%20card (2022)
31. Shukla, S.: RBI in final stages of retail CBDC pilot rollout. https://economictimes.indiatimes.com/: https://economictimes.indiatimes.com/news/economy/policy/rbi-in-final-stages-of-retail-cbdc-pilot-rollout/articleshow/95598347.cms?from=mdr (2022)
32. Telefonica: Metaverse and cryptocurrencies, what is their relationship? Retrieved from Telefonica: https://www.telefonica.com/en/communication-room/blog/metaverse-and-cryptocurrencies-what-is-their-relationship/amp/ (2022)
33. TOI: Waiting for Cabinet approval, says finance minister on bill on cryptocurrency. Times of India. https://timesofindia.indiatimes.com/business/india-business/waiting-for-cabinet-approval-says-finance-minister-on-bill-on-cryptocurrency/articleshow/85373759.cms (2021)
34. Vidal-Tomás, D.: The illusion of the metaverse and meta-economy. Int. Rev. Financ. Anal. **86**, 102560 (2023)
35. Wang, Y., et al.: A survey on metaverse: fundamentals, security, and privacy. IEEE Commun. Surv. Tutorials **25**(1), 319–352 (2023)
36. Wilson, C.: Cryptocurrencies: the future of finance? In: Tony Yu, F.-L., Kwan, D.S. (eds.) Contemporary Issues in International Political Economy, pp. 359–394. Springer, Singapore (2019). https://doi.org/10.1007/978-981-13-6462-4_16
37. Worldcoin.org: Why Is Cryptocurrency Important? How Is It Revolutionizing the World? Retrieved from worldcoin: https://worldcoin.org/articles/why-is-cryptocurrency-important#:~:text=The%20revolution%20of%20cryptocurrency%20is,without%20a%20central%20third%20party (2022)
38. Qaroush, Z., Zakarneh, S., Dawabsheh, A.: Cryptocurrencies advantages and disadvantages: a review. Int. J. Appl. Sci. Smart Technol. **4**(1), 1–20 (2022). https://doi.org/10.24071/ijasst.v4i1.4610

Research on the Application of Metaverse Technology in the Field of Intelligent Transportation

Mengke Hu and Liangbin Cheng[✉]

School of Marxism, Huazhong University of Science and Technology, Wuhan 430074, China
{d201981189,chengliangbin}@hust.edu.cn

Abstract. The combination of metaverse and transportation provides new infinite possibilities for the future development of intelligent transportation. The metaverse-empowered intelligent transportation has the characteristics from single to multiple dimensions, from reality to virtual-real co-prosperity, from high-carbon to low-carbon, and has been widely used in disaster accident simulation, car driving skills training, traffic and travel game experience, Maas and other fields. At the same time, the metaverse faces challenges in the application of intelligent transportation, such as incomplete policies and regulations, threats to information security, and monopolies in data sharing. While making good use of the metaverse to bring development opportunities to intelligent transportation, it is also necessary to further improve policy supervision systems, data sharing systems, and information protection mechanisms to prevent potential impacts and risks.

Keywords: Metaverse · Intelligent Transportation · Application Scenarios · Development Strategies

1 Introduction

Currently, humanity is in the 3.0 era of rapid development in network information technology, and the metaverse is also thriving in various industries. The metaverse provides infinite possibilities for the development of intelligent transportation, and empowering intelligent transportation by the metaverse has become a new development trend in the field of transportation. The ways and means of human communication are no longer limited to the use of physical transportation, but are beginning to change to the information field and virtual world.

Although the term "Metaverse" has only become active in the public vision in recent years, it can be traced back to 1992, when science fiction writer Neal Stephenson first proposed it in his book *Snow Crash* and described it as a virtual world parallel to the real world, where everyone can find their human identity. In the social field, with Facebook changing its name from "Facebook" to "Meta" in October 2021, it instantly brought the metaverse into the public vision. Subsequently, in March 2022, the successful listing of the first metaverse concept stock, Roblox, further propelled the metaverse to the

S. He et al. (Eds.): METAVERSE 2023, LNCS 14210, pp. 98–107, 2023.
https://doi.org/10.1007/978-3-031-44754-9_8

forefront of the market. At present, with the popularization of intelligent devices and the continuous maturity of technology, the development of the metaverse is accelerating. Driven by practical needs and the feasibility prospects of constructing the metaverse, the metaverse has attracted more and more attention from around the world.

Metaverse is built on the integration of virtual reality and augmented reality technologies, achieving multimodal interaction between virtual environments, digital elements, and humans [1]. In the metaverse, people can still live and work normally, but everything is virtual. With the rapid transformation of production methods and the continuous progress of science and technology, the mode of mobility starts to develop in the direction of intelligence, gradually changing from foot-based to intelligent terminals based on "data" and "computing power". The Metaverse has the potential to redefine urban mobility and service to improve the efficiency of urban mobility and environmental quality. BMW, Mercedes-Benz, Hyundai and many other automotive giants have announced that they have entered the Metaverse era and are exploring the application of the metaverse in the field of intelligent transportation. At the same time, Chinese automakers are also actively exploring the field of the metaverse. At the end of December 2021, BYD successfully applied for the registration of the "BYD Metaverse" trademark, which is internationally classified as a means of transportation. The 2022 Song Pro DM-i has some characteristics of the "metaverse" and is known as China's first "metaverse" concept car.

2 The Basic Characteristics of Metaverse Empowered Intelligent Transportation

The metaverse has broken the absolute isolation in geographical space, causing people to move from the "visible and tangible" real world to the "visible and intangible" virtual world. As a future development trend in the field of transportation, the combination of the metaverse and intelligent transportation presents basic characteristics of moving from single to multiple dimensions, from reality to virtual-real co-prosperity, from high-carbon to low-carbon. The metaverse has changed the sense of mobility experience that people can only get by being in it, achieving a sense of perception of the world without leaving home, providing infinite possibilities for the development of human mobility.

2.1 From Single to Multiple Dimensions

On the one hand, in terms of technology, the combination of metaverse and intelligent transportation has realized the integration from a single technology to multiple technologies. The rapid development and application of science and technology have brought humanity into the era of intelligence, and the importance of technology in various fields around the world is increasingly prominent. The application of new generation information technology, represented by big data, artificial intelligence, digital twin, virtual reality (VR), 5G, etc.in the transportation field has long been common and has become a technological dependence for the high-quality development of the transportation industry. For example, the development and use of digital twin technology [2] in automotive equipment power and transmission systems; virtual reality (VR) and augmented reality (AR) [3] provide immersive 3D experiences; the application of artificial intelligence technology in comprehensive traffic management; the application of big data technology in road detection; 5G communication technology improves ultra-high reliability and ultra-low latency services for intelligent transportation, among others. But with the appearance of metaverse, it means the integration of these single technologies and application scenarios, forming a comprehensive intelligent transportation system with multiple technologies, multiple application scenarios and multiple application fields, realizing the multifaceted integration of transportation and metaverse at the underlying technology level, and helping to push transportation towards a more intelligent, safe and green direction.

On the other hand, in terms of resources, the combination of the metaverse and intelligent transportation has achieved effective integration of multiple resources. The metaverse is a multidimensional digital space, and the transportation system is a complex and comprehensive system involving multiple resources. The combination of the metaverse and intelligent transportation not only achieves multi-dimensional integration of natural resources such as coal, oil, air, land, and social resources such as human and information, but also assists in the coordinated scheduling of cross transportation systems such as highways, waterways, railways, and urban public transportation. In the metaverse, not only can we enjoy physical world mobility services through digital subscriptions, but we can also effectively supplement composite energy by converting oil and gas to electricity, electricity to light, and other means, solving regional differences in energy production and consumption, and effectively improving resource utilization efficiency[4].

2.2 From Reality to Virtual-Real Co-prosperity

Traditional transportation refers to the use of various means of transportation in physical space to meet people's mobility needs, while intelligent transportation in the metaverse can plan and choose the optimal mobility mode and route for people through the integration of virtual and real data, and even enable people to complete their real-world mobility needs in virtual space without leaving their homes. For example, BMW Group combines metaverse technology with existing digital twin factories, integrating artificial intelligence and metaverse into its own production through the use of the NVIDIA Omniverse, making its digital factories more efficient and intelligent [5]. In other words, in the Omniverse platform, BMW managers and manufacturers can design and plan vehicles in a virtual world, which will break the boundaries of time and space, bringing real-world designers together in the virtual world so that engineers around the world can design and validate simultaneously in different locations at the same time. In addition, the vehicle road testing and collision testing have also been moved from the real world to the virtual world. Designing and testing vehicles in the virtual world can not only optimize the experimental process, improve work efficiency, but also minimize production costs caused by actual assembly and verification. At the 2023 CES exhibition, BMW also launched the i Vision Dee concept car, which, as its latest digital achievement, can intuitively express the emotional interaction between people and cars, effectively integrating the emotional experiences of drivers in both the virtual and real worlds. In addition, Nissan has introduced the concept of Invisible-to-Visible (I2V), which uses a 3D augmented reality interface to merge the real world with the virtual world. On the one hand, combining the information collected by sensors inside and outside the vehicle with data from Nissan's Omni Sensing Cloud provides drivers with information on road environmental conditions and potential hidden obstacles or pedestrians, enabling them to see "invisible" information. On the other hand, the metaverse connects drivers and passengers to a virtual world where family, friends and others from around the world can appear in the car as 3D images through mixed reality (MR) technology, enabling communication and interaction in both time and space [6].

2.3 From High-Carbon to Low-Carbon

The emergence of the metaverse not only strengthens monitoring of environmental pollution and reduces carbon emissions, but also has a significant impact on achieving other global climate goals. Most traditional modes of transportation are powered by oil, kerosene, and diesel. High emission and high pollution motorized transportation emits a large amount of harmful substances such as carbon dioxide and nitrogen dioxide into the air, causing irreversible and serious damage to the ecological environment. The intelligent transportation empowered by metaverse "the core of its response to climate change is its ability to reduce the demand for mobility" [7], will realize real-time monitoring of air environment, exhaust emissions, noise pollution, etc. through ubiquitous sensor systems, and establish a digital space combining reality and reality between ecological environment and transportation, so as to realize energy saving and emission reduction in the field of transportation. For example, virtual characters and travel scenes can be created for travelers in the metaverse world, so that travelers can intuitively experience the comfort and carbon emissions of different modes of transportation, and prompt them to choose low-carbon and environmentally friendly travel modes; virtual space can also be used to simulate and integrate multiple modes of transportation, achieving effective connection between different modes of transportation, and reducing resource waste and environmental damage caused by repeated construction. In addition, in the virtual world created by the metaverse, humans can reduce the demand for mobility because they can apply physical places to virtual environments to meet their mobility experiences and needs, reducing the frequency of mobility in the real world. The reduction of travel frequency and demand also means that the use of oil and other energy will decline, so as to reduce energy consumption and greenhouse gas emissions generated by mobility consumption, and achieve the goal of carbon neutrality. In addition, the energy and resources in the virtual world will be stored and used as virtual products, shared by countless people, without consuming or damaging their quantity and quality [7].

3 The Application Scenarios of Metaverse Empowered Intelligent Transportation

Under the empowerment of the metaverse, intelligent transportation is no longer a means of transportation to meet people's mobility needs, but gradually becomes an intelligent tool for social interaction and leisure entertainment. Its economic value and social functions are also increasing. Metaverse empowering intelligent transportation refers to the application of underlying technologies through intermediaries to various mobility scenarios. The underlying technologies represented by VR, AR, MR, 5G, big data, etc. are the foundation for the widespread application of the metaverse in intelligent transportation. The intermediary level, mainly composed of device hardware and platform software, is the technology carrier for various application scenarios to be realized, and the combined effect of the two meets the travel needs of users at the user level (Fig. 1). With the emergence of the metaverse, the relationship between underlying technologies and upper-level users has also been further deepened.

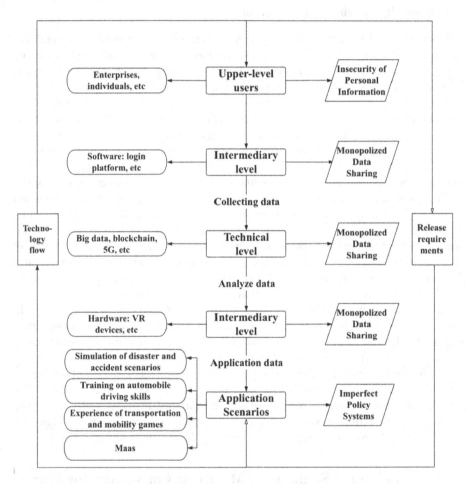

Fig. 1. The technical architecture of metaverse empowering intelligent transportation

3.1 Simulation of Disaster and Accident Scenarios

In the digital virtual space of the metaverse, traffic data can be collected through sensors and transmitted to algorithms for data analysis, simulating natural disasters and major traffic accidents in advance and conducting immersive exercises. Although collecting data in real life is both expensive and time-consuming, it is not the case in the metaverse. In the metaverse, blockchain technology can be used to efficiently and quickly collect and process data. The use of metaverse technology to simulate disaster and accident scenarios can not only provide people with repeated simulations and drills, help them better allocate materials and rescue personnel, but also timely summarize experience, scientifically plan rescue plans, set up emergency plans, and improve corresponding infrastructure construction to improve their ability to handle and solve unexpected situations, and minimize more personnel and property losses.

3.2 Training on Automobile Driving Skills

The metaverse establishes a dynamic world that combines the virtual and the real, simulating driving situations in various road environments so that drivers can feel the driving experience of different road environments and traffic conditions, thus improving the driver's response ability and adaptability to different events, especially for the training of large vehicle drivers. For example, Waymo has built a virtual world – Simulation City to test the performance of its autonomous vehicle. In this virtual world, realistic simulations are used to minimize the gap with the real world to ensure that the vehicle can respond to all problems encountered on the real road in a timely manner, to improve Waymo Driver's learning ability, emergency handling ability, and to validate new software, and also to increase the driver's confidence in driving the car in the real world to a certain extent [8].

3.3 Experience of Transportation and Mobility Games

Under the empowerment of the metaverse, intelligent transportation also allows users to fully experience mobility products and services through immersive gaming experiences in the virtual world. For example, Hyundai Motor Group launched the metaverse game "Hyundai Mobility Adventure" on the metaverse platform Roblox as early as October 2021 [9]. In virtual space, users can freely transform into different roles and complete various tasks related to travel solutions by driving different styles of modern cars. Users can also engage in various social activities through dressing up virtual images, upgrading garages, and other forms. At the end of 2022, Porsche also launched its first cloud-based amusement park – "Porsche Dream City", creating a cloud-based interactive scene in a metaverse virtual environment.

3.4 Mobility as a Service (MaaS)

The typical application scenario of metaverse empowering intelligent transportation is MaaS. MaaS is a diversified, personalized, and intelligent social comprehensive system that integrates functions such as itinerary reservation, route planning, and online payment, providing users with a one-stop and immersive experience, and paying more attention to seamless user mobility experience. In the MaaS system, users will purchase corresponding mobility services based on their mobility needs, rather than just transportation. As the first company in China to introduce an integrated mobility service platform, Gaode will also consider it as the first project in 2023. It can be seen that the one-stop travel service platform established in the metaverse environment has strong spatiotemporal scalability, strong economic value, social value, and ecological value, which will have a disruptive impact on the traditional transportation and travel field.

4 The Possible Challenges of Metaverse Empowered Intelligent Transportation

As an emerging technology, the development of the metaverse is in a gestation period of pressure accumulation and weight bearing progress. The concept of empowering intelligent transportation by the metaverse is worthy of recognition and is also the direction of future transportation development. However, with the application and development of new technologies such as metaverse, artificial intelligence, and 5G, the traditional automobile mobility industry has undergone tremendous changes, while also exposing many thorny problems. The development of metaverse in intelligent mobility has a long way to go.

4.1 Insecurity of Personal Information

The metaverse is a more open digital space, and personal information security will also be greatly threatened [10]. The amount of data collected in metaverse will far exceed that of the internet today. In the virtual world, users can collect human biological information such as eye tracking information, gesture information, electroencephalogram, electromyogram, etc. through wearing virtual and augmented reality devices [11]. This information is easily abused, causing personal information leakage and threatening users' privacy rights. For example, some advertisers obtain personal information through illegal transactions, accurately identify target customers based on user behavior habits, preferences, and other data, and promote their products and advertisements. With the continuous application and popularization of the metaverse, if user personal information is not protected, the abuse and illegal trading of user information will only become increasingly common, and the security of user personal information will also be seriously threatened, even causing infringement on the personal and property security of users.

4.2 Monopolized Data Sharing

Data is a core resource advantage and competitive advantage for metaverse enterprises, and data sharing has become the foundation for data development and utilization by major intelligent transportation enterprises. Nowadays, driven by maximizing profits, automobile companies are prone to data monopoly, data abuse, and data leakage. The early and mature leading metaverse vehicle companies have a huge consumer flow and data resources, which play a crucial role in further enhancing user stickiness, exploring potential users, and achieving precise push. However, some companies are unwilling to share relevant technologies and data in order to seize the market and pursue economic benefits, often building a "data isolation wall", forming a typical data monopoly in the metaverse field. This behavior has limited the entry of other automotive companies into the metaverse field, which is not conducive to stimulating enterprise and market vitality.

4.3 Imperfect Policy Systems

As an emerging technology, the metaverse is still in its infancy and normative stage, and the relevant policies and systems are not yet sound. Although China has issued relevant regulations and policies to support the development of new transportation modes such as shared mobility and new energy vehicles, there is no clear regulatory scheme or regulation to protect the application of metaverse in intelligent transportation. At the same time, intelligent transportation under the empowerment of the metaverse emphasizes user participation and experience, while the formulation of policies and laws has a certain lag, and the relevant regulations are often issued only after the problems appear, which lacks certain foresight and effectiveness. In addition, there are still serious challenges in how to better implement the application of the metaverse in intelligent transportation, clarify the responsibilities of relevant regulatory departments, and clarify the responsibilities of various economic entities.

5 Suggestions for the Development of Metaverse Empowered Intelligent Transportation

Promoting the healthy and orderly development of intelligent transportation empowered by the metaverse is an inevitable trend in the development of new digital transportation, and an effective path to address climate change and promote sustainable economic and social development. Therefore, it is necessary to propose corresponding countermeasures and suggestions for the potential challenges that the metaverse may encounter in intelligent transportation, in order to constrain and standardize the industry order that the metaverse empowers intelligent transportation, minimize potential risks, stimulate the positive role of metaverse technology in intelligent transportation, and fully leverage the social value of data for the benefit of humanity.

5.1 Improving a Scientific and Efficient Policy Supervision System

Firstly, it is necessary to timely incorporate the empowerment of the metaverse and intelligent transportation into relevant policies, and continuously formulate and improve relevant regulations and policy requirements. The introduction of policies should be based on the original intention of "preventing problems before they occur", and in response to the possible situations and contradictions that may arise in the development of intelligent transportation in the metaverse, relevant regulations and policies should be formulated and introduced in advance to achieve legal compliance in the first time. Secondly, at the national level, it is necessary to strengthen supervision, raise the entry threshold for metaverse vehicle enterprises, stabilize the market competition pattern, provide correct guidance on business management rules and other aspects, promote industry standardization and sustainable development, and create a good development environment. Third, governments at all levels should accelerate the establishment of a new model of "Internet + supervision", and establish a more standardized, accurate and intelligent supervision system integrating online and offline with big data, cloud computing, artificial intelligence and other technologies. Supervise the development of metaverse empowering intelligent mobility through remote supervision, real-time supervision, and timely control enterprises that operate in violation of regulations to rectify market chaos and effectively safeguard the legitimate interests of various economic entities.

5.2 Creating a Standardized and Orderly Data Sharing System

Firstly, the country needs to enhance its control capabilities for data security in empowering intelligent transportation in the metaverse, establish a data security supervision platform, standardize data trading behavior, strictly supervise the data trading process, strictly eliminate data monopoly behavior, always be vigilant about the breeding of data hegemony, and form an open and orderly data sharing situation. The second is that relevant enterprises in the metaverse empowering intelligent transportation should establish and improve data management systems and operating procedures, and consciously and compliantly share data. To further ensure the security, confidentiality, and authenticity of the data itself, and to ensure the legality and compliance of the data sharing process. Thirdly, in the process of empowering intelligent transportation in the metaverse, individuals should enhance their awareness of data security, pay attention to their own data security, enhance their awareness of data security prevention, and be cautious about the "default options" in data usage rules to avoid personal data leakage caused by time saving.

5.3 Establishing a Secure and Reliable Information Protection Mechanism

One is to accelerate the legal protection of personal information in empowering intelligent mobility in the metaverse. We should establish and improve the legal protection system for personal information in the metaverse field as soon as possible, improve the protection of personal information under existing laws, clarify the responsibilities and obligations of information collectors, and ensure the right of information subjects to know and choose their own information usage. The second is to strengthen the supervision of information security in the empowerment of intelligent mobility in the metaverse. Clarifying the main regulatory authorities for information security, strengthen supervision before, during, and after the event, improving the accountability mechanism for regulatory authorities, and truly achieving accountability. The third is to increase the punishment for the misuse and resale of personal information in the application of intelligent mobility in the metaverse. Strictly crack down on illegal disclosure and sale of personal information, and truly play the warning role of the punishment mechanism.

6   Conclusion

In the process of promoting the development of intelligent transportation, the metaverse contributes to the development of intelligent transportation with its unique technological and social value. By focusing on the emerging products and services of the metaverse, it can be seen that the metaverse has the characteristics of moving from single to multiple dimensions, from reality to virtual-real co-prosperity, from high-carbon to low-carbon in

intelligent mobility. At the same time, it has broad application prospects in disaster accident simulation, car driving skills training, transportation game experience, Maas, and
other fields. However, as an emerging technology, the development of the metaverse is
not yet mature, and its application in intelligent transportation also faces challenges from
policy systems, data technology, information security, and other aspects. It is necessary
to further establish and improve policy supervision systems, data sharing systems, information protection mechanisms, etc. to ensure the deep integration of the metaverse and
intelligent transportation. For the metaverse and intelligent transportation, their exploration and development are only at the beginning. Only by discovering and solving
problems through continuous development, and establishing a link between the metaverse and intelligent transportation, can intelligent transportation continue to develop
for the better with the support of the metaverse.

Acknowledgment. This research was supported by Research on the Ministry of Education's 2021
General Project for College Teachers of Ideological and Political Theory Courses: Research on
the Ideological and Political Improvement of Teaching 'An Introduction to Natural Dialectics'
(NO. 21JDSZK048).

References

1. Pamucar, D., Deveci, M., Gokasar, I., Tavana, M., Köppen, M.: A metaverse assessment
   model for sustainable transportation using ordinal priority approach and Aczel-Alsina norms.
   Technol. Forecast. Soc. Chang. **182**, 1217789 (2022)
2. Batty, M.: Digital twins. Env. Plann. B: Urban Anal. City Sci. **45**(05), 817–820 (2018)
3. Gaffary, Y., Le Gouis, B., Marchal, M., Argelaguet, F., Arnaldi, B., Lécuyer, A.: AR feels
   "softer" than VR: haptic perception of stiffness in augmented versus virtual reality. IEEE
   Trans. Vis. Comput. Graphics **23**(11), 2372–2377 (2017)
4. Zhao, G., Zhang, Q., Li, H.: Research on the development trend of China's internet of vehicles
   under the background of Metaverse transportation. Logistics Eng. Manag. **45**(02), 64–70
   (2023)
5. BMW Group: BMW Group and NVIDIA take virtual factory planning to the next level.
   https://www.press.bmwgroup.com/global/article/detail/T0329569EN/bmw-group-and-nvi
   dia-take-virtual-factory-planning-to-the-next-level?language=en (2023)
6. Nissan: https://www.nissan-global.com/EN/INNOVATION/TECHNOLOGY/ARCHIVE/
   I2V/. 23 Mar 2023
7. Allam, Z., Sharifi, A., Bibri, S.E., Jones, D.S., Krogstie, J.: The metaverse as a virtual
   form of smart cities: opportunities and challenges for environmental, economic, and social
   sustainability in urban futures. Smart Cities **5**(03), 771–801 (2022)
8. Voinea, G.D., et al.: Study of social presence while interacting in metaverse with an augmented
   avatar during autonomous driving. Appl. Sci. **12**(22), 11804 (2022)
9. Hyundai. Hyundai Motor Vitalizes Future Mobility in Roblox Metaverse Space, Hyundai
   Mobility Adventure. https://www.hyundai.com/worldwide/en/company/newsroom/hyundai-
   motor-vitalizes-future-mobility-in-roblox-Metaverse-space%252C-hyundai-mobility-adv
   enture-0000016713 (2023)
10. Falchuk, B., Loeb, S., Neff, R.: The social metaverse: battle for privacy. IEEE Technol. Soc.
    Mag. **37**(2), 52–61 (2018)
11. Zhang, C.: The challenges and responses of the development of the metaverse to personal infor-
    mation protection – also on the conceptual reconstruction of personal biometric information.
    Law Forum **38**(02), 132–141 (2023)

Metaverse Applications for Construction of Educational Digital Resources

Kunjing Zhang[✉]

Shenzhen Institute of Information Technology, Shenzhen 518172, Guangdong, China
2013100916@sziit.edu.cn

Abstract. The application forms, existing problems and development trends of the metaverse oriented to the construction of educational digital resources are studied. This study can enrich the form of education, improve the efficiency of learning, and has a good application prospect, which needs further research. Through case studies and literature studies, this paper explores how to better accomplish teaching objectives, improve the effectiveness of educational effect evaluation, make students' participation traceable, achieve diversification of resource development forms, and break through the restrictions of education popularization. In the metaverse application for the construction of educational digital resources, it is necessary to pay attention to learners' sense of user experience, improve students' participation and learning efficiency, help teachers better display course content, and promote knowledge exchange, collaboration, creation and sharing. This research will help to explore and apply metaverse technology to improve the existing education model, promote the transformation of digital education, enhance educational experience, deepen disciplinary research, cultivate educational digital talents, and promote the innovation and transformation of the education industry.

Keywords: Metaverse · digital education · education technology · educational digital resources · educational model

1 Introduction

Metaverse is a new type of network space that perfectly integrates virtual world and real world, and serves as a future virtual social network based on the real world with digital world as medium, and supported by technologies such as artificial intelligence, augmented reality, and virtual reality.

1.1 Conducting Research on Metaverse Applications for Construction of Educational Digital Resources Is of Great Significance and Value for the Future Development of Education, Mainly for the Following Reasons

(1) **Enriched educational forms:** Traditional teaching methods are mainly focused on classroom teaching and field experience. By applying metaverse technology

to education, it can greatly expand the forms and carriers of education – providing more virtual environments, interactive experiences, and innovative teaching methods, offering learners diversified learning choices and promoting educational effectiveness.

(2) **Open educational resources:** Metaverse technology can bring together educational resources from different places and times into virtual platform, making resource sharing easy to accomplish, enabling students to interact with classmates and teachers from all around the world. This resource sharing spirit plays a significant role in revolutionizing the field of education, assisting in the rapid spread of high-quality educational resources, even for free and open access, thereby promoting equitable and balanced development of education. The difference between learning resource sharing and MOOC is that learners can have more immersive learning experience when learning on the metaverse learning platform and better communicate with teachers and students in the same time and space.

(3) **Improved learning efficiency:** Digitally constructing educational resources using metaverse technology can improve learning efficiency. By applying highly realistic virtual scene simulations and interactive scenario-based case design, learners can better understand key knowledge points, resulting in increased learning efficiency and autonomy. Today's young students are the digital generation, and they are full of curiosity and love for virtual reality teaching. In order to improve learning efficiency, educators need to do a good job in design and guidance.

(4) **Promising prospects:** Metaverse technology is among the trends of the future digital economy era, with extremely wide application scenarios and potential. In terms of education-oriented applications, introducing metaverse technology will help students embrace digital culture, train their adaptive ability to future technology environments, master new network information technology, and lay a solid foundation for their career development.

Therefore, conducting research on metaverse applications for construction of educational digital resources will have far-reaching impacts on promoting digital education, social progress, talent cultivation, and industrial markets.

1.2 The Research Goal of this Paper is to Explore and Apply Metaverse Technologies to Improve Existing Educational Models. Specifically, How to Effectively Increase Student Engagement and Learning Efficiency by Introducing the Metaverse into Learning, Help Teachers Better Present the Course Content, and Promote Knowledge Exchange, Collaboration, Creation, and Sharing. In Addition, this Study Addresses the Following Research Objectives:

(1) Reveal the theoretical and practical significance of metaverse technology under the development background of educational digital resources.

(2) Explore how to better apply metaverse technology to different levels and fields of educational environments to strengthen the integration of education digitization and informationization.

(3) Summarize best practices in metaverse application, develop optimal usage strategies and solutions and address issues that teachers and students encounter during the application process.

2 Research Status

Currently, the construction of digital education resources is rapidly developing globally. Research achievements on the construction of digital education resources are constantly being published in academia. However, there are not many studies combining the meta-universe technology with the development of digital resources. The following are some of the main current situations of metaverse application research for the construction of digital education resources both domestically and internationally.

Internationally
The study of the metaverse began in developed western countries, such as the United States, Germany, and South Korea. Scholars from these countries have conducted relevant in-depth research and published numerous academic achievements. Several famous universities in the United States, such as the University of California, Berkeley and University of Michigan, Ann Arbor, are also exploring innovative educational approaches by further breakthroughs and applications of metaverse technology. Representative viewpoints related to research and practice of metaverse application in digital education resource construction include:

(1) To deepen the concept of metaverse into the field of education and creating an innovative education mode. Ting develops a comprehensive Edu-Metaverse ecosystem architecture which provides an effective implementation reference for the development of the Edu-Metaverse [1].
(2) A large number of related policy documents have been issued and implemented successively, promoting the popularity and development of digital education resources and online education.It closely integrates the virtual and real worlds in terms of the economic system, social system, and identification system and allows users to produce content and edit the world [2, 3].
(3) Various well-known universities and companies have launched various online education platforms based on artificial intelligence and the Internet era, and conducted in- depth exploration combining with course design, development, and training work [4–10].
(4) The development of digital education resources and technology applications continues, involving various types of learning support tools such as games, virtual reality, simulation software, ERP systems, etc. [11–13].
(5) Networked cross-school courses, global educational projects, and jointly established MOOCs are also quietly emerging, enriching transnational education cooperation [14, 15].

In China
In the early stage, research and practice of the metaverse in China were concentrated in the field of "natural sciences". For example, in 1994, the Computer School of South China

University of Technology first introduced virtual experimental software into graduate education and became one of the first universities in China to carry out related research.

In recent years, with the rapid development of VR/AR technology, China has realized the huge potential of the metaverse, and the educational application of the metaverse has received more and more attention and research. Several related companies (such as Huawei, 360, Shenzhen Xunfei Intelligent Technology, etc.) have actively entered this field.

At the same time, mainstream education systems have begun to attach importance to digital construction, and some domestic universities (such as Southern University of Science and Technology, Beijing University of Technology, etc.) are gradually applying the metaverse to education.

The current situation of research and practice of metaverse application for educational digital resources construction in China includes the following representative viewpoints:

(1) The Chinese government attaches great importance to the digital transformation of education, and successively formulates more comprehensive and transparent policy documents, and invests heavily to promote the allocation and application of various educational resources.

(2) The new online education has gradually become popular in national universities, and has developed into an important online teaching medium. Whether it is online classrooms or technologies such as intelligent recognition, cloud preparation, live Q&A, they are becoming increasingly widely applied.

(3) The school's academic affairs departments strengthen layout and better establish a digital education resource platform in cooperation with teachers, aiming to improve the level of education and alleviate the burden on teachers.

(4) Various feedback-type App software continues to innovate and improve. Apps in multiple fields, such as word science popularization and encyclopedia, can also expand innovation in information filtering, visual optimization, and increasing interaction. At the same time, App related to student psychological suggestion can cultivate many effective factors to build a healthier educational ecosystem through personalized mechanisms such as ghostwriting.

(5) Some new technologies are also becoming popular, such as augmented reality (AR) and virtual reality (VR), which have become effective expansions of educational resources and brought more intuitive and vivid learning methods.

(6) In terms of digital resource construction, there is still a large gap and imbalance in the construction of various links and content resources, especially in the construction of educational resources in rural areas.

In summary, the construction of educational digital resources worldwide is currently in a period of rapid development. From clear policies to technological innovations, from talent training to rich resources, various factors are actively promoting the future popularity and development of digital education. However, there are still many problems and challenges in the construction process, such as fairness, completeness of knowledge system, and security, which require the cooperation of all participants to solve. Scholars at home and abroad have made many attempts to solve these problems and challenges and have achieved some experience and results worth learning and reference. Based on the research results of predecessors, this article will conduct an in-depth study and exploration of the high interactivity, collaboration, creativity, and knowledge sharing characteristics reflected in the online educational resources empowered by metaverse technology, and explore how to better improve educational effectiveness and social benefits with metaverse technology.

3   Methods

This study mainly adopts case study and literature review methods.

(1) Case study method

Analyze and research the actual application effects and status of metaverse technology in the high-quality online open resources courses of the Shenzhen Institute of Information Technology in China. Explore the significance and reasons through in-depth descriptions and analysis of the case.

(2) Literature review method

Through studying existing literature, discuss the issues and challenges of metaverse applications in the digital resource environment for education, based on relevant theories, technological principles, and applications of metaverse.

In summary, by utilizing different research methods mentioned above, this study aims to explore the application of metaverse technology for educational digital resource construction, which will facilitate high-quality research results and promote the process of digitization in education.

4   Results

The following are the research results of metaverse application for educational digital resource construction:

(1) **Improved effectiveness of education evaluation:** developing virtual learning environments based on scenario simulation using metaverse technology can help understand students' learning status, comprehension level, and knowledge absorption capacity. It is expected to evaluate the teaching effectiveness under different resources and scenarios with real data, providing a more effective reference basis for fine-tuned teaching strategies.

(2) **Trackable student participation:** Metaverse applications can also collect visual sensor statistical data to track student behavior, interaction, and reactions in virtual scenarios. This data can further analyze value information such as student preferences and interests, helping education professionals shift their focus from merely teaching content to an all-round perspective that takes into account student needs and teaching effectiveness.

(3) **Exploration of resource development forms:** Metaverse applications require early resource investment, including scene model design, animation production, audio creation, character setup, etc. Research focuses on large-scale resource-sharing models, detailed resource production guidelines, and more practical operation strategies, exploring efficient production and community-based cost optimization for digital educational resources under metaverse application.

(4) **Overcome education accessibility limitations:** Metaverse technology has a wide range of applications, but factors such as technical barriers and funding constraints make it difficult to achieve high coverage and penetration rates. This study adopts collaborative measures for different participants such as schools, teachers and parents, providing diversified support and assistance, and timely proposing adjustments to the best path plan to reach feasible and unified demonstrations.

This study provides a reference basis for the digital transformation and future development trends of the education field, promoting continuous innovation and improvement of metaverse applications for educational digital resource construction to play a more important role in the education field.

5 Discussion

5.1 What are the Ways in Which Effective Use of the Metaverse Can be Applied to Education?

(1) **Virtual Lab:** Using metaverse technology to construct a virtual lab allows students to perform various experimental operations in the virtual world, effectively improving students' practical skills and theoretical knowledge. The virtual lab is of great help for practices on high-precision equipment because such devices are generally costly and easy to make mistakes, but through the metaverse virtual lab, it can better reduce costs, provide students with more trial and error opportunities, and ultimately improve their professional skills and practical level.
(2) **Virtual Classroom:** Building a virtual classroom in the metaverse and completely porting offline courses to the virtual world, synchronous online teaching and interactive learning activities can be carried out in the virtual classroom, making it easier for students to participate and learn freely. In the years where COVID-19 was severe, the virtual classroom played a prominent role, allowing teachers and students to gather in a virtual classroom for mutual communication and learning, without being affected by distance or viruses that disrupt learning schedules and results. At the same time, it also realizes the digital split technology, which allows students to study different courses and attend different meetings at the same time. In order to avoid the use of digital dopes in virtual classes, teachers can detect whether students are listening through interactive features that ask the whole class questions (such as a question for them to choose or answer), just like traditional classroom questions.
(3) **Virtual Museum:** Establishing a virtual museum in the metaverse, demonstrating museums' collections, historical and cultural landmarks digitally, allowing students to gain an in-depth understanding of the related knowledge, and participating in interactive visits. We all know that immersive learning is more conducive to students' appreciation of knowledge. Still, it's challenging to achieve large-scale, full-coverage immersive learning and visits in real life. However, the virtual museum in the metaverse can provide immersive teaching experiences for all students, visit some places that are impossible to visit in real life, experience the unique cultural heritage brought by cultural relics, and feel the weight of history.We know that virtual museums are a very mature field, but virtual museums in the metaverse will

be more traceable, allowing learners to visit data at a glance, and more helpful for educators to guide and motivate learners to study and visit purposefully.

(4) **Virtual Professional Training:** Applying virtual training to vocational education, such as using virtual factories as experimental parts of product quality control courses or using metaverse technology to simulate hospital computer system operations training. Taking China's vocational education as an example, every semester has a week of time dedicated to professional training. In reality, to avoid too many students using the training room simultaneously, causing inadequate resources, schools stagger trainer usage. Still, through the metaverse virtual professional training, it would be more convenient to implement. It can be deployed uniformly, arranged uniformly, and conducted online for professional practice teaching and training, making teachers and students more relaxed, thus having more energy available for learning and practical aspects of their profession, without worrying about time and space issues.

(5) **Virtual Social Platform:** Using metaverse to build a communication platform, inspiring knowledge sharing and creativity improvement among students or teachers, such as setting up virtual learning groups and playing different roles to conduct various theme communication and interaction. The educational resource online platform empowered by the metaverse is not only a platform for learning knowledge but also a virtual social platform for students to communicate, socialize, and interact with each other. Students with common interests and hobbies from different schools may discuss a particular topic, which can better stimulate students' learning enthusiasm, explore questions, and solve problems, which are benefits that traditional teaching does not have. Existing technologies may not provide visitors with a friendly and smooth virtual experience, but with the development of network bandwidth and hardware technology, virtual social communication in the metaverse will become a way of life.

The metaverse has great potential for broad applications in education. By creating virtual laboratories, classrooms, museums, professional training, and social platforms, we can greatly improve students' learning interest and effectiveness, promote educational innovation, and advance the future of educational models.

5.2 Although the Metaverse Has a Wide Range of Applications in the Field of Education, There Are Still a Series of Challenges and Limitations in Digital Resource Construction, Including

(1) **Resource costs:** Building a complete metaverse requires significant investment in design, development, and operation costs, which affects resource usage and optimization. To implement educational applications in the metaverse, a large number of high-quality educational resources need to be gathered, especially 3D virtual scene resources with good interactive effects. This requires a substantial investment of funds and time, and technical issues such as computing power and data processing also need to be addressed, ensuring resource production efficiency, quality, and safety.

(2) **(2) Technical support:** Currently, metaverse technology is still in the stage of continuous exploration and improvement, and the existence of technical bottlenecks limits

its speed and depth of application in the field of education. Metaverse technology is still in its early stages of development and has not been widely adopted. Educational institutions require support from diverse talent resources, such as excellent software developers, senior education experts, etc., to promote the organic integration of digital education resources and metaverse technology. However, general educational institutions lack the independent technology and capability to develop metaverse spaces and can only realize the construction and use of educational spaces through purchasing services. For example, the main subject of this study, Shenzhen Information Polytechnic, achieved the construction of the metaverse virtual museum education space by buying technical services from professional companies. Building a high-quality, content-rich metaverse that accurately reproduces real life and ensures good interactivity requires substantial resource investment and professional personnel maintenance.

(3) **User experience:** In order to make users truly willing to use metaverse technology for education and learning, in addition to providing rich digital materials and interactive features, smooth interfaces and user-friendly interfaces must be provided. In the past, the educational presentation method was dominated by the classroom, but under the situation where the information flow gradually loses its control, it may not necessarily be widely accepted to convert university education into a digital teacher based on the metaverse. Educational institutions should carefully consider the real demand and maturity of the education population in promoting the process of creating a digital community of shared future and focus on promoting diverse educational models while effectively retaining their core values.

In the teaching practice of the research group, I deeply felt the importance of user experience. Taking our school as an example, in the space access of the educational digital resources metaverse, which is similar to a virtual museum built by our school, nearly 50% of the students gave up the access during a learning task because the access time had to wait for about 10 s (loading resources), and 8% of the students visited for less than 1 min (Fig. 1).

Visit duration	Sessions	Share
0seconds	253	49.51%
1-5seconds	4	0.78%
6-10seconds	5	0.98%
11-30seconds	12	2.35%
31-60seconds	21	4.11%
1-3 minutes	67	13.11%
3-10 minutes	149	29.16%
10-30 minutes	0	0%
More than 30 minutes	0	0%

Fig. 1. Visit duration

In terms of browsing pages, only 13% of students view more than five pages (Fig. 2).

Page view	Sessions	Share
Browse only 1 page	253	49.51%
Browse 2 pages	96	18.79%
Browse 3 pages	48	9.39%
Browse 4 pages	30	5.87%
Browse 5 pages	17	3.33%
Browse pages 6-10	39	7.63%
Go to pages 11-20	28	5.48%
Go to pages 21-50	0	0%
Browse more than 50 pages	0	0%

Fig. 2. Page view

These user experience data also made our team a little disappointed, and did not achieve the teaching goals and effects we wanted. Therefore, in the construction of optimizing educational resources, we must pay attention to user experience, expand server bandwidth, improve access efficiency, set clear access tasks and assessment objectives, effectively extend students' access time and browse the number of pages, in order to achieve the teaching objectives and effects we want.

(4) **Privacy and intellectual property protection**: Since metaverse technology and related application services also face the problem of network security and data privacy, the user information protection mechanism and security requirements should be strengthened in the construction of educational resources. In addition, the virtual scenes, models and other resources involved in the metaverse application are open to the public, so it is very important to protect intellectual property rights. Unauthorized appropriation, dissemination of confidential educational content, malicious modification of scenes and other violations will pose a threat to the security of educational resources. Therefore, it is necessary to strengthen the constraints of rules and regulations and design relevant practical operation methods to ensure the quality of resources.

Overall, as a new virtual social network, the application of the metaverse in the construction of digital education resources faces multiple challenges. However, with continuous technological innovation and improvement, we believe that these limitations will gradually be overcome, and the metaverse will become one of the important forces driving the development of digital education. To solve the above problems, the solution proposed in this article is to unite various educational institutions and universities to jointly invest funds and manpower to build a shared metaverse space. This approach can solve financial problems, reduce construction costs, expand the benefits, and concentrate the strengths and resources of various universities to solve technical problems and achieve better user experiences by co-building, sharing, and developing metaverse spaces.

5.3 The Future Development Trend and Direction of Metaverse Applications in Digital Education Resource Construction Mainly Manifest in the Following Aspects

(1) **Establishment of open standards:** In order to promote the interconnection of metaverse platforms, the industry needs to establish open standards for the metaverse to achieve more flexible and convenient user experience in the absence of unified protocols.

(2) **Good user design experience:** With the growing demand for VR/AR technology, the future metaverse will focus on improving user experience and enhancing learning and teaching effects.

(3) **Parent or teacher as supervisory role:** As internet usage increases, parents and teachers will increasingly become excellent participating regulation institutions in the virtual world, protecting personal information security, and preventing violence and other issues.

(4) **Big data analysis:** Through the application of big data and AI technology, the metaverse platform can conduct data analysis and mining based on students' learning trajectories, thereby providing more suitable educational resources and methods for different student groups.

(5) **Simulation scenarios:** Simulated scenarios based on virtual reality technology have become one of the most promising fields for metaverse applications in the education sector. In the future, the construction and optimization of virtual scenarios will be given more emphasis in the construction of metaverse educational digital resources.

In summary, with continuous technological innovation, the metaverse will play an increasingly important role in enhancing student learning experience, improving teaching quality, expanding knowledge domains, accelerating information sharing, and driving the development of digital education into a new stage.

6 Conclusion

The research on metaverse applications for digital education resource construction has significant practical value and theoretical significance, and its main value is manifested in the following aspects:

(1) **Promoting the transformation of digital education:** Metaverse technology lays an important foundation for establishing a close connection between digital educational resources and actual teaching. The research results can assist in achieving universal education and innovation of digital education modes, promoting the realization of more diversified forms of education, from traditional classroom teaching to virtual 3D interaction, and continuously launching various education products and services.

(2) **Upgrading the educational experience:** The application of metaverse represents a significant breakthrough in providing personalized teaching methods. Leveraging metaverse tools can make student learning more efficient and enjoyable. Through corresponding experiments and evaluations, the research results can open up more opportunities for improving the student learning experience, tapping into student potential, and cultivating their skills and abilities.

(3) **Further deepening subject research:** Metaverse applications can provide strong support for practices in various knowledge fields. Research on the field of educational technology can continue to iterate on functionality and characteristics, even attracting collaboration from other academic fields. At the same time, this new digital education platform can create conditions for cross-disciplinary research and academic exchanges, and form a good environment for spiritual infusion and creative exploration.

(4) **Developing digital education talent:** With the development of metaverse applications, more professionals in related careers such as scene model design, animation production, audio creation, and character setting will have opportunities for advancement. The research results can also provide a basis for cultivating advanced talents in the education field, encouraging and supporting them in exploring innovative education solutions, and promoting the modernization and development of education.

The research on practical issues of metaverse applications in the education sector is of great significance for promoting the transformation and innovation of the education industry. The research results can fully tap into its potential value and tremendous advantages, and provide irreplaceable impetus for the future development of education systems and quality work.

Acknowledgements. This research was supported by 2021 Guangdong Provincial. Youth Research Project: Research on the value goal and path innovation of young. Marxists in the new era (No. 2021GJ047).

References

1. Wu, T., Hao, F.: Edu-Metaverse: concept, architecture, and applications. Int. Interact. Learn. Environ. (2023)
2. Lan, G.S., Wei, J.C., Huang, C.Y., Zhang, Y., He, Y.T., Zhao, X.L.: Learning meta-universe enabling education: building a new mode of "intelligence+" education application. J. Mod. Distance Educ. **40**(2), 35–44 (2022)
3. Zheng, X.D.: Smart education 2.0: the new ecology of education from the perspective of education informatization 2.0. J. Mod. Educ. **36**(4), 11–19 (2018)
4. Hua, Z.X., Huang, M.X.: Research on teaching field structure, key technology and experiment of educational meta-universe. Mod. Distance Educ. Res. **33**(6), 23–31 (2021)
5. Yuan, F., Chen, W.D., Xu, R.Y., Ge, W.S., Zhang, Y.F., Wei, H.M.: Scene empowerment: perspectives on scenario based design and its educational applications. J. Distance Educ. **40**(1), 15–25 (2022)
6. Zhong, Z., Wang, J., Wu, D., Zhu, S., Qin, S.Z.: Application potential and typical scenarios of educational met averse. Open Educ. Res. **28**(1), 17–23 (2022)
7. Hua, Z.X., Fu, D.M.: Study the connotation, mechanism, structure and application of the metaverse. e J. Distance Educ. **40**(1), 26–36 (2022)
8. Chaiyarak, S., Koednet, A., Nilsook, P.: Blockchain, computing for smart education management. Int. J. Educ. Inf. Technol. **14**, 52–61 (2020)
9. Goyal, M.K., Varshney, S., Dubey, P.: Internet of Ting based smart education environment. J. Crit. Rev. **7**(9), 1372–1376 (2020)

10. Dou, J.H.: The reconstruction of teaching ecosystem under the concept of smart education. J. Heilongjiang Teach. Dev. Coll. **40**(11), 42–44 (2021)

11. Gao, T.G., Du, J., Wang, N.: Research on ecological construction of school wisdom education. China Electron. Educ. **12**, 26–32 (2021)

12. Liu, G.P., Gao, N., Hu, H.L., Qin, Y.C.: Educational metaverse: characteristics, mechanism and application scenarios. Open Educ. Res. **28**(1), 24–32 (2022)

13. Fu, W.X., Zhao, W.L., Huang, H.D.: An empirical study on embodied learning effectiveness in the field of education meta-universe. Open Educ. Res. **28**(2), 85–95 (2022)

14. Zhai, X.S., Zhao, X.Y., Wang, M.J., Zhang, Z.W., Dong, Y.: Education meta-universe: innovation and challenge of the new generation of Internet education. Open Educ. Res. **28**(2), 34–42 (2022)

Author Index

Printed in the United States
by Baker & Taylor Publisher Services